COOPERATIVE DISCIPLINE

Linda Albert, Ph.D.

American Guidance Service, Inc.
Circle Pines, Minnesota 55014-1796

Cooperative Discipline Contributing Authors

Pete DeSisto, M.Ed.
   Former District Administrator, Broward County, Florida;
   International Education Consultant
Patricia Kyle, Ph.D.
   Author; Assistant Professor of Counseling Education, University of Alaska,
   Anchorage; International Education Consultant
Andy LePage, Ph.D.
   Author; International Education Consultant
Marilyn McGuire, M.S.
   Author; School Administrator, Bellevue, Washington;
   International Education Consultant
Will Roy, Ph.D.
   Associate Professor of Curriculum and Instruction, University of
   Wisconsin, Milwaukee; International Education Consultant
Frances Smith, Ph.D.
   Principal, Big Springs Elementary School, Richardson, Texas; Instructor,
   Principal's Academy of the National Association of Elementary School
   Principals; National Education Consultant
Al Soriano, M.S.
   Supervisor of Leadership Training, Hillsborough County Public Schools,
   Tampa, Florida
Yvette Zgonc, M.Ed.
   Author; Licensed Mental Health Counselor; Parent Educator;
   International Education Consultant

Karen Dahlen, *Associate Director*
Maureen Wilson, *Director of Creative Services*
Marjorie Lisovskis, *Editor*
Charles Pederson, *Assistant Editor*
Evans McCormick Creative, *Design and Typesetting*
John Bush, *Cartoons*
Terry Dugan, Terry Dugan Design, *Cover Design*

Printed in the United States of America

Library of Congress Catalog Card Number 95-77062

ISBN 0-7854-0042-7

Product Number 4073

A 0 9 8 7

*To my son, Steven Moraff,
with much love and appreciation
for the richness you bring
to my life*

CONTENTS

PREFACE

I wrote this revised edition because I'm even more of an idealist today than I was six years ago. Despite growing discipline problems and escalating violence in our schools and society, teachers are increasingly finding Cooperative Discipline an antidote to these and other ailments they face in the classroom. The success stories teachers have shared with me are an abiding ray of hope, convincing me more than ever that the Cooperative Discipline approach does provide answers to our questions about managing classrooms and motivating students to choose cooperative behavior.

What's new in this expanded version of *A Teacher's Guide to Cooperative Discipline?* Additional intervention and encouragement strategies for working with *all* students. Instructions for developing a classroom code of conduct and conflict resolution procedures. Many added strategies for including students, parents, and others in the discipline process. A focus on violence and gang prevention. An emphasis on helping students with special needs—including those from different geographic and social cultures—succeed in the regular classroom.

Many wonderful people gave freely of their time to help in the preparation of the original version of this book: Nancy Berla, Betty Lou Bettner, Lynn Bounds, Mary Bullerman, Stan Dubelle, Amy Lew, John Lizer, John Lucas, Al Mance, Cameron Meredith, Sue Mihalik, Edna Nash, Sharon Robinson, and Barbara and Robert Turk.

This new edition was further aided by the insights and contributions of Ercell Binns, Lois Brewer, Claudia Bricks, Phyllis Davis, Pat Evans, Louise Griffith, Betty Hollas, Kris Halverson, Esther Klein, Jodi Lamb, Barry MacDonald, Barbara McClamma, Stephanie Meegan, Marti Monroe, Tina Oxer, Ruth Pridgen, Maryanne Roesch, Joann Spera, Cindy Tucker, Patricia Voss, Dane Ward, and Marti White.

A number of talented editors took my words and made them flow in an organized, readable manner: Judith Rachel, Lois Welshons, Judy O'Donnell, and Margie Lisovskis. Thanks also to John Bush for his charming cartoons; Carol Evans, Keith McCormick, and Nancy Condon for their clear and direct page design; and Terry Dugan for his cover design.

Anyone who lives with a writer has to be a little crazy. Writers wail when they are blocked. They throw temper tantrums when deadlines approach too soon. Through all these travails—on both editions of this book—my husband, Byron Eakin, has stood by me: encouraging me when I was down, pushing me when I was stuck, and bolstering my confidence when I ceased to believe that I could ever finish these pages. Thank you, Byron, for being my guiding light. And, once again, I promise to give you a breather before I start another writing project. Even crazy people have limits.

INTRODUCTION
The Approach: Practical and Positive

Since writing the first edition of the *Cooperative Discipline* teacher's guide in 1989, I have traveled across the country—north, south, east, and west—introducing the Cooperative Discipline approach to teachers and administrators. With each new group, I've heard a recurring concern. Teachers are overwhelmed by the special challenges they face: escalating numbers of students categorized as emotionally or behaviorally disordered, escalating class size coupled with the mainstreaming of special-needs students, escalating demands on teachers to fill nonteaching roles in children's lives. They are frightened by the increasing incidence of severe classroom disruptions and violence and by the toll this is taking on teachers and students alike.

The teachers I've met have tried all kinds of approaches. They have used behavior modification and assertive techniques. When these failed to produce the promised results, some even resorted to permissiveness. Yet the problems keep rising. It's clear that teachers everywhere are hungry for an effective approach to classroom discipline that can help them gain control of their students, their classrooms, and their jobs.

It has been a source of pride and satisfaction for me to share with these teachers the success stories of their contemporaries: teachers who have taken on the Cooperative Discipline approach as their own, using and adapting it to help them manage their classrooms, build caring relationships with students, and instill in their students a spirit of responsibility, cooperation, and mutual respect.

To put it simply, Cooperative Discipline shows teachers how to work hand in hand with students, colleagues, and parents to solve the discipline dilemma. With *cooperative* as the byword, two achievements are possible: First, the classroom becomes a safe, orderly, inviting place in which to teach and learn. Second, student self-esteem increases, which must happen if we want students to behave more responsibly and achieve more academically.

Too good to be true? Not if we take into account that we, as teachers, have enormous power in influencing our students' behavior. When you use the corrective, preventive, and supportive strategies described in the pages that follow, you'll join the ranks of teachers who have harnessed this enormous power for the benefit of their students, themselves, and the entire school community.

Students won't always remember what we teach them, but they will never forget how we treat them.

The Key: Quality of Teacher-Student Interaction

Determining exactly what students expect from us and what we expect from students is the key to creating positive classroom behavior. Teacher-student interaction is a two-way street: The students relate to us, and we relate to them. When students choose to relate to us through misbehavior, we have to be able to recognize the purpose, or the *goal*, of the misbehavior and know how to respond to it both immediately and in the long term.

Teachers have enormous power in influencing students' behavior.

Cooperative Discipline provides teachers with the skills necessary to identify the goal of a particular misbehavior and with specific intervention techniques that can be used at the moment of the misbehavior. It also looks beyond the teacher-student interaction brought about by the misbehavior, suggesting practical ways to create future positive interactions that build mutual respect and trust.

Cooperative Discipline offers a process that's corrective, supportive, and preventive. Most of us would acknowledge that intervention techniques alone provide only temporary relief; we can depend on a recurrence of the misbehavior. On the other hand, if we couple intervention with steps for building self-esteem and mutual respect, we'll usually achieve positive relationships with our students and, consequently, appropriate behavior that lasts.

The Goal: Cooperative Relationships in and Beyond the Classroom

The Cooperative Discipline approach encourages a positive relationship not only between teachers and students but also with parents, other teachers, and administrators. Achieving such cooperation is not an easy task. When misbehavior is an issue, parents, students, teachers, and administrators often play the "blame game." They tend to point the finger at one another, or at contemporary influences such as popular song lyrics and movie themes, or at social problems such as unemployment, child abuse, and drug abuse. Even gangs may be blamed as the cause rather than viewed as a symptom of the problem. This blame game has no winner; every player's token remains stuck on the problem, rather than moving forward to achieve active solutions.

Educators, parents, and students play the blame game for a variety of reasons. Perhaps they feel powerless in the face of what seems to be an overwhelming problem. Perhaps they believe they can't control detrimental influences in the modern world. Perhaps they don't think they personally can make a difference. Perhaps they don't want to admit that they don't know what to do next.

Cooperative Discipline suggests alternatives to the blame game by showing concretely how parents, students, and educators can work together to solve discipline dilemmas. It provides specific suggestions on how to establish workable partnerships that can make a difference in behavior no matter what environmental factors are at work.

The blame game has no winners.

The Framework: Time-Tested and Practical

Cooperative Discipline represents a synthesis of theories about behavior and discipline translated into practical skills and strategies. The theories are up-to-date, respected ideas about human development, communication, and cooperation that can be applied in today's diverse classrooms. Since young people reflect the values and behaviors that they see around them, they must be approached with modern methods for effective discipline.

Forming the theoretical framework of this book are the philosophy and psychology of Alfred Adler and Rudolf Dreikurs as well as compatible theories of William Glasser, Albert Ellis, and Eric Berne. Their ideas have been tested and refined by thousands of educators and are used successfully by many other professionals, from therapists to business consultants. They help people live and work together harmoniously.

Cooperative Discipline is also based on my own experiences as a classroom teacher and on ideas I've exchanged with classroom and special education teachers throughout the country while presenting discipline workshops. The original book was refined on the basis of evaluations from teachers and administrators in twenty school districts (representing urban, suburban, and rural settings) and with the aid of two advisory boards, one composed of educators and the other of students. The current updated and revised version of the *Cooperative Discipline* teacher's guide reflects comments, suggestions, and additional strategies recommended by teachers who have implemented its principles in their classrooms and schools. Their insights and ideas greatly enhance the scope and effectiveness of the Cooperative Discipline approach.

The Action Plan Process: Theories Become Practice

No discipline approach can be effective unless its theories can be put into practice. Within the Cooperative Discipline approach, theories are translated into a useful diagnostic, corrective, and prescriptive tool—the Action Plan Process. The process enables teachers to develop an individualized discipline plan specific to a student's needs. It also provides a vehicle for involving colleagues, administrators, parents, and the students themselves in the development of the plan.

The School Action Plan helps teachers determine how to interact with a particular student. We develop the plan to guide our behavior toward a student so that we can respond to the student's misbehavior with reasoned effort rather than in a reflexive manner. This School Action Plan can be developed with the assistance of other teachers, administrators, and support-service personnel. Why go it alone when we're surrounded by colleagues whose advice and encouragement can make all the difference in the world?

The Home Action Plan shows interested parents and guardians how to apply the Cooperative Discipline strategies at home so that young people are receiving a consistent message at home and at school.[1]

You don't have to go it alone! Cooperative Discipline lets you build a collaborative climate for working with students, parents, and other school personnel.

The Student Action Plan brings students into the loop, forcing them to confront their own misbehavior and to commit themselves to more appropriate behavior choices in the future.

Each of these action plans is based on the same steps:

1. Pinpoint and describe the student's behavior.
2. Identify the goal of the misbehavior.
3. Choose intervention techniques for the moment of misbehavior.
4. Select encouragement techniques to build self-esteem.

An important outcome of all the action plans is the demonstration of belief in the student's ability to behave in responsible, cooperative ways.

The Winner: The Entire School Community

Everyone wins when Cooperative Discipline is implemented.

Teachers Teachers gain the knowledge and skills to cope with classroom disruptions that previously drove them to distraction. As the daily discipline struggles decrease, satisfaction in teaching increases. As they learn how to build and strengthen quality relationships with their students, teachers feel better not only about students but about themselves. The potential for teacher burnout is greatly reduced.

The Cooperative Discipline approach is useful for teachers of all levels, from kindergarten through high school. It applies in urban, suburban, and rural communities and in public, private, and parochial settings. The basics of behavior and the dynamics of teacher-student interactions remain constant no matter what level the teacher's experience or what age the student.

What *does* change according to student age is the applicability of intervention and encouragement techniques. Therefore, Cooperative Discipline includes a variety of techniques appropriate for various age groups.

Students Students also are winners in the Cooperative Discipline process. Students are almost as upset as the teacher when misbehavior disrupts a class. Students want to learn in an orderly, firm-yet-friendly classroom atmosphere. When they have that opportunity, their academic performance is likely to rise. Moreover, their self-esteem is nurtured as their teacher employs the encouragement strategies that are basic to Cooperative Discipline.

Teachers using Cooperative Discipline happily report that the program is effective with at-risk and special education students, with the "difficult child" and the gang "wanna-be." The consistency of structure and response, as well as the focus on creating a climate that enhances self-esteem and satisfies the strong psychological and emotional need to belong, makes Cooperative Discipline appropriate for *all* students in *all* settings.

Parents Parents benefit from the Cooperative Discipline process too. They gain confidence and optimism from knowing that their child's school behavior is being guided according to a specific, carefully constructed plan of action. Many family adults also welcome the opportunity to participate in the Cooperative Discipline process by developing and carrying out a Home Action Plan that parallels the School Action Plan.

A consistent focus on structured choices, self-esteem, and belonging make Cooperative Discipline appropriate for all *students in* all *settings.*

Getting Started: The Process Unfolds

The chapters that follow explain the Cooperative Discipline process, both in theory and practice. Reading the chapters consecutively is recommended because they build on one another. The discussion of the basics of behavior in Chapters 1-3 is necessary to following the process effectively. After that, we can begin the practical process, which involves taking objective, corrective, supportive, and collaborative action as we develop a School Action Plan.

As the Cooperative Discipline process unfolds, you will explore these major topics:

- what students are trying to achieve when they misbehave
- what intervention techniques to use at the moment of misbehavior
- how to reinforce desirable behavior
- how to create a cooperative classroom climate that reduces disruptions and prevents violent behavior
- how to avoid and defuse confrontations and resolve conflicts cooperatively
- how to use encouragement to build mutual respect and student self-esteem
- how to use the Action Plan Process to develop individualized discipline plans
- how to involve colleagues, administrators, parents, and students as partners in the discipline process

One last word. Cooperative Discipline isn't a panacea that will solve all classroom discipline problems instantly. Rather, it's a process to follow over time for constructing creative, positive, and personalized solutions to discipline problems. Success depends on you and the dynamics of your powerful influence on your students' lives.

Note

1. Additional information on involving parents can be found in the booklet *Bringing Home Cooperative Discipline* (Circle Pines, MN: American Guidance Service, 1994) and in the videotape program *Responsible Kids in School and at Home: The Cooperative Discipline Way* (Circle Pines, MN: American Guidance Service, 1994).

As teachers, each of us has wrestled with certain questions about student behavior over and over again: How can I convince misbehaving students to stop what they're doing? How can I inspire well-behaved students to continue to cooperate? How can I motivate passive, underachieving students to respond and apply themselves academically?

The answers to these questions begin with an understanding of three basic concepts of behavior, concepts with implications all teachers must understand if they are to be effective with all students:

1. Students choose their behavior.
2. The ultimate goal of student behavior is to fulfill the psychological and emotional need to belong.
3. Students misbehave to achieve one of four immediate goals.

This chapter and the two that follow explore these concepts in detail.

Choices, Choices, Choices

Dan is routinely tardy for English class and usually hands in assignments late. Why? Leroy is always willing to do work for extra credit. Why? Emily mutters four-letter words under her breath during geometry. Why? Sumiko is always the first to volunteer to stay after school to help with classroom tasks. Why? The answer is simple: Because they choose to behave in this way.

Many social scientists suggest far more complex explanations of behavior: that it is based on childhood experiences or on heredity, environment, instinctive needs, or conditioned responses. Such hypotheses, however true or false, do not help us maintain discipline in the classroom. Dan's teacher can't do anything to change Dan's early childhood experiences. Leroy's enthusiasm for extra credit may be prompted by his father's promise of a dollar for every A on his report card. His teacher can't easily change the father's means of motivation. Emily's teacher can't change the DNA of Emily's cells. Sumiko's impulse to help may be the result of her reluctance to go home to an unhappy situation. Her teacher can't change Sumiko's home life.

Reminding ourselves that behavior is based on choice can give us some strategic leverage.

As teachers, we can't change a student's life outside of school, any more than we can go back into a student's past to right a wrong.

Understanding that behavior is based on choice, however, can provide us with strategic leverage in coping with it.

Consider Emily: In her first-period English class she pays attention and contributes to discussions. Her English teacher describes Emily as a "bright, cooperative, alert girl who relates well to her peers." An hour later, in geometry class, Emily mutters obscene words, talks out of turn, and refuses to complete assignments. This teacher describes Emily as a "nuisance who disrupts my teaching and distracts other students."

Does Emily's family environment change between first and second period? Do her genes shift? Of course not. In both classes, Emily *chooses* behaviors that make sense to her—although not necessarily to her teacher. The proof that Emily chooses her behavior is that she behaves differently in different situations.

Do rules make students choose positive behavior? How we wish that were the case! Almost all students know both the classroom and school rules and, if asked, could recite them forward and backward. When six-year-old Coty runs in the hall, has he forgotten the rule about walking? When fifteen-year-old Tessa saunters into class five minutes after the bell, has she forgotten the rule about being on time? No. Coty and Tessa have *chosen* to "forget" the rules. Coty's teacher can tell him to stop running in the hall until she's blue in the face, but Coty won't stop running until he *chooses* to walk. The decision to change is Coty's alone; the rule exists, but neither the rule nor the teacher's repetition of it can make Coty choose to obey it.

No one and no situation can *make* anyone behave in a certain way. Though people, events, and conditioning may invite a particular behavior, the invitation can be accepted or rejected. The choice exists. Once we understand that behavior is based on choice, we can begin to influence a student's decisions about how to behave. The change starts with us. We need to learn how to interact with students so they will want to choose appropriate behavior and comply with the rules.

How conscious are students of the choices they are making? No one knows for sure. However, I have interviewed dozens of secondary students in front of large groups of teachers, asking them to identify classrooms where they behave appropriately and where they misbehave. These young people, who have often been chastised, sent to the office, and even suspended, are typically very clear about being in control of their choices and in identifying the circumstances that influence them.

What about students with learning disabilities and attention-deficit disorders? Isn't their behavior neurologically determined? Again, there is no definitive answer. What is known, however, is that—no matter what the origin of their behavior—these students must learn to make appropriate behavior choices and to be accountable for the choices they make if they are to succeed in school and life.

Let's look, then, at some of the major factors that influence the choices students make.

All students have the potential for moving toward positive behavior choices.

Teacher Expectations

Cooperative Discipline is built on the premise that all students have the potential for moving toward more positive choices of behavior and for becoming responsible citizens of the school community. This is true regardless of students' heredity, background, gender, race, ethnic origin, or current level of functioning.

Research and experience show that "what you expect is what you get." Teachers who expect that all students can learn tend to have classrooms full of eager, successful learners. Similarly, teachers who expect that all students can make positive behavior choices tend to create classrooms where appropriate behavior is the norm, not the exception.

How we view students who misbehave influences our expectations. If we see them as "bad" or as kids who have something "wrong" with them, we tend not to expect much improvement. When we see in their cumulative folders a long history of behavior problems, our low expectations seem to be confirmed. We might be tempted to think it's impossible to teach these children to make positive choices.

We can raise our expectations by describing misbehaving students as students with a "choosing disability"—an underdeveloped ability to choose appropriate behavior. Understood in this way, our challenge is similar to the task we face to help children with reading disabilities or speech impediments. We remediate a choosing disability by individualizing our approach to each student, selecting our methods and materials based on the student's demonstrated needs, and choosing from a variety of remedial techniques available. The chapters that follow will show us how.

Expectations and past experiences can sometimes cloud our perceptions and keep us from seeing the positives.

Styles of Classroom Management

The behavioral choices students make are greatly influenced by the style we choose to use in managing our classroom: permissive ("hands-off"), autocratic ("hands-on"), or democratic ("hands-joined").

The Hands-Off Style

In recent years the permissive, *hands-off* style of management—a hallmark of the "free" school movement—seems to have disappeared from the educational scene. Experience proved that with neither clear boundaries nor immediate, effective teacher interventions at the moment of misbehavior, many students pushed the limits and continued to make poor behavior choices. Teachers who adopted the hands-off style often were reacting against the autocratic, hands-on style, not realizing that a more effective alternative exists.

The Hands-On Style

When students misbehave and the class seems to be getting out of control, a hands-on style of discipline can seem extremely appealing. Why not "make" students behave? Isn't obedience to laws that we lay down preferable to the chaos and disruptions that interfere with teaching? What's wrong with telling students to "do it because I say so" and expecting that they'll comply? After all, many of us had teachers who used this style, and it seemed to work. Many of us, in fact, have used the hands-on style ourselves and probably found that it used to be relatively successful.

What, then, is wrong with hands-on discipline? Why can't we continue to use autocratic methods to control and discipline students? Because the students who are most troublesome in our classrooms choose their worst behaviors when faced with teachers who use the hands-on style of management. They confront, rebel, and subvert the teacher's best efforts to maintain order. In the words of one high school student from New York, "No teacher's gonna boss me around. I can make them more miserable than they can make me." Equally if not more important, this same student behaved cooperatively for other teachers who used a different style of management.

"You cannot shake hands with a clenched fist."
—Indira Gandhi

The Hands-Joined Style

Most administrators have had the experience of moving a student from the classroom of Teacher A, where the student is sent to the office day after day, to the room of Teacher B, who doesn't seem to have the same difficulties with the student. The usual explanation is that a "personality conflict" exists between the student and Teacher A. The real explanation is that Teacher A uses a hands-on management style, which influences the student to make poor choices, while Teacher B uses the hands-joined style, which has the opposite effect.

What is the magic in the hands-joined style? Why are schools that are involved in the Quality School and Quality Teaching movement using this style? For a clear and simple reason: Because research and experience have shown that when students are respectfully treated as important decision-makers who have the right to make choices and participate in the design of their education, they behave more cooperatively and achieve more academically.[1]

In many ways, the hands-joined style of classroom management is site-based decision making at the classroom level. We know that effective schools are those in which teachers are included in the decision-making process. Effective classrooms are those in which students are included in the decision-making process and therefore are strongly influenced to develop responsibility and choose cooperative behavior.

Obviously, Ms. Whippet doesn't understand why the hands-on approach isn't working.

Teacher Responses to Misbehavior

When students misbehave, it's natural for teachers to feel upset and angry. After all, we're distracted from what we've been hired to do—teach! Our confidence in our ability to maintain an orderly classroom is threatened. How we deal with these feelings, and the responses we make to misbehavior, greatly influence what students will do next.

While we can't control the students and force them to behave in certain ways, we *can* control ourselves and our actions. It's important to remain unimpressed and adopt a businesslike attitude when faced with poor behavior choices. Our relaxed body language and calm, yet firm, tone of voice convey to students that we're in charge of ourselves and of the situation. From this stance, we can begin to build a hands-joined classroom of responsible, cooperative learners.

Note

1. William Glasser, "The Quality School," *Phi Delta Kappan* 71 (no. 6):424-35.

CHAPTER 2
The Basics of Behavior 2: The Need to Belong

People live in social groupings—the home, the school, the workplace. We can't survive without one another. Since students spend at least six hours a day in school, their ability to find a satisfying place in the classroom group is of major importance.

What It Means to Belong

There's more to belonging than simply occupying a physical place in a classroom. The need to belong refers to the strong psychological and emotional need all students have to feel important, worthwhile, significant, and valued. Satisfying the need to belong is as basic to our psychological well-being as is satisfying the need to breathe to our physical well-being.

Given the diverse composition of today's classrooms, it's of paramount importance to pay attention to this need to belong. It's all too easy for members of minority groups to feel excluded from the mainstream of classroom life and to develop unproductive attitudes and disruptive behaviors as a result.

Even a violent existence may be motivated by the need to belong. Most gang members report their affiliation is prompted by the "family" the gang provides.

The Importance of the "Three Cs"

To experience a strong sense of belonging in school, students must satisfy Cooperative Discipline's "Three Cs."[1] They need to feel *capable* of completing tasks in a manner that meets the standards of the school. They need to believe they can *connect* successfully with teachers and classmates. They need to know they *contribute* to the group in a significant way.

Students seek to satisfy the Three Cs in the way that makes the most sense to them at the time. When they believe they are unable to be capable, to connect, or to contribute by behaving appropriately, they may try to achieve their goal of belonging by misbehaving. Three factors affect students' ability to satisfy the Three Cs in the classroom:

- the quality of the teacher-student relationship
- the strength of the classroom climate for success
- the appropriateness of the classroom structure[2]

The Three Cs:
Capable
Connect
Contribute

With these factors in mind, consider again the divergent behaviors of Emily in first-period English and second-period geometry. What happens in English class? Emily and her English teacher have a positive relationship based on mutual respect. (Emily *connects*.) She experiences a sense of success in her English classwork. (She feels *capable*.) She can learn and exchange ideas within the classroom structure that's been established. (She *contributes*.) Emily behaves appropriately because her English teacher's classroom lets her satisfy the Three Cs positively.

In contrast, Emily is unable to satisfy the Three Cs positively in geometry class, so she chooses to satisfy them through misbehavior. She connects in an uncooperative manner but nonetheless forces her teacher to relate to her. She satisfies her need to feel capable by refusing to do assignments; after all, if she did them and failed, she would feel incapable. Unfortunately, the structure of the class prevents Emily from taking the opportunity to contribute in any significant way.

Emily's Jekyll-and-Hyde behavior is typical. Most of us know students with such dual behaviors. The need to belong also explains why some young people exhibit behavior at school that's markedly different from their behavior at home:

> *Angelica's teacher had looked forward to meeting her mother at parent-teacher conferences. He introduced himself and said, "I want to compliment you, Mrs. Rosetti. Angelica is one of the most courteous and cooperative children I've ever taught." Mrs. Rosetti raised her eyebrows in surprise. "You must have the wrong folder on your desk!" she exclaimed. "My daughter drives everyone batty at home, and she never cooperates!"*

Clearly, Angelica has found positive ways to live up to her name at school. But she has been unable to discover how to feel capable, how to connect, and how to contribute at home. As a result, parent and teacher are experiencing contrasting behaviors.

We've also observed students who consistently behave or misbehave. In the same classroom, we have students who continually choose to work and learn with us along with students who choose not to. All these students have the same ultimate goal—to fulfill their need to belong by satisfying the Three Cs. Once we become aware of this need, we can help the satisfied students continue to feel satisfied. And we can help the dissatisfied find positive, appropriate ways to achieve satisfaction.

Young people choose different behaviors to feel significant in different groups—the family, the class, the neighborhood, the friendship group, the ball team, the band, the youth group, even the gang. When we recognize this need to belong, we're on our way to helping students choose appropriate behavior to achieve their special place in our classroom.

It's tempting to focus on how we can change the student who misbehaves. The encouragement process is a far better—and easier—place to start!

The Encouragement Process

With Cooperative Discipline you will learn a variety of specific Three C strategies, many of which take very little time or effort to implement. I call the implementation of the Three C strategies the *encouragement process*.

Teachers benefit in many ways when they use encouragement in their classrooms. The more we encourage students, the less they choose to misbehave. Why? Because they don't have to act out to get us to notice them. We've given them the gift of our attention and shown that each of them is a valued member of the class. When we generously use encouragement to help students feel capable, connected, and contributing, they have nothing to prove, no need to confront us.

Perhaps no factor that influences how students choose to behave is as important as the amount of encouragement students receive from a teacher. When every interaction between a student and a teacher leaves the student feeling capable, connected, and contributing, the great majority of behavior choices that the student makes will be positive. This positive response to authentic encouragement occurs regardless of the student's culture, background, or innate ability.

Encouragement is the most powerful tool we possess.

Encouragement and Self-Esteem

Research in education tells us that students with healthy, resilient self-esteem achieve more academically and cause far fewer behavior problems than students who lack self-esteem. Therefore it benefits us as teachers to do everything possible to boost our students' self-esteem.

The good news is that the encouragement process fosters self-esteem. Students feel good about themselves—and about their ability to succeed in school—when they believe they are *capable* learners who can *connect* in positive ways with classmates and teachers and find ways to *contribute* to the class and the school.

Encouragement and Violence Prevention

Unfulfilled needs lead to anger, frustration, and feelings of powerlessness. These feelings often erupt in young people—especially those who have never learned safe outlets for such emotions. The more we use encouragement to meet students' basic psychological and emotional needs, the fewer outbursts we'll face in the classroom.

Much of the violence we see in the classroom reflects the increasing amount of violence we see everywhere in society. Nevertheless, the amount of violent behavior seen in schools *decreases* when encouragement is as much a part of daily life as reading, writing, and arithmetic.

Encouragement and Gang Prevention

Some young people are not able to satisfy their need to belong in school, at home, or in their neighborhood with socially acceptable behavior. Often these young men and women join gangs. When we consider how, unfortunately, a gang can satisfy the Three Cs, it's not hard to understand why this happens.

In a gang, everyone learns to feel *capable*—capable of carrying out the gang's orders because each gang member is taught to do what's expected. In a gang, everyone is *connected*—by such things as colors, clothing, handshakes, and graffiti. In a gang, everyone is given responsibilities and expected to *contribute* to the "good" of the group.

If we wish to eliminate gangs from our schools and neighborhoods, we must join together as a community to create a social environment where young people feel capable, connected, and able to contribute. Our classrooms, schools, and neighborhoods must become places where the Three C climate exists for all children and young adults.

Encouragement and Inclusion

Current educational policies require that students with special needs be placed in the least restrictive environment. When placed in regular classrooms, these students have the same need to belong as others. The same encouragement strategies are equally applicable to these students and will have the same beneficial effect on their self-esteem and on the behavior choices that they make.

Inclusion succeeds best when the classroom climate is built on encouragement.

Inclusion will succeed best when the classroom climate is built upon the Three Cs. Rather than focusing on academic and behavioral deficiencies, Cooperative Discipline's encouragement process emphasizes strategies that:

- Build each student's belief that "I can do it."
- Help every student form positive relationships with teachers and classmates.
- Allow all students to contribute to the class group in their own unique ways.

Encouragement for All

Encouragement is for everyone. As a teacher once told me, "If you don't feed the teachers, they will eat the children." Teachers, especially, need a whopping dose of encouragement every day. The daily challenges we face require extraordinary courage, dedication, and commitment. Encouragement is the sun that warms the heart of everyone in the school community. It's free. It's healthy. It isn't even fattening!

When we recognize and nurture the need to belong, we're on our way to helping students choose appropriate behavior to achieve their special place in our classroom.

The more encouragement you give, the more you'll get back. So extend the Three C strategies beyond the walls of your classroom—to colleagues, administrators, parents, friends, and family. Savor the encouragement you receive in return. Use it to nourish yourself so you can in turn nourish the students whose lives you touch every day.

Notes

1. The Three Cs are adapted from a concept developed by psychotherapist-educators Amy Lew and Betty Lou Bettner.
2. Linda Albert, *Coping With Kids and School* (New York: Dutton, 1984), 115.

CHAPTER 3
The Basics of Behavior 3: The Four Goals of Misbehavior

Not every off-task behavior is a misbehavior that requires disciplinary action. Before we put the Cooperative Discipline intervention strategies to use, we must first ask ourselves two questions:

- Is the level of instruction on this particular task appropriate for this student?
- Are the methods, materials, and pacing I'm using to teach this lesson appropriate for this student?

Once we're able to answer yes to these questions, we can feel assured that it's time to put Cooperative Discipline interventions into action. Let's define misbehavior as anything students do that interferes with our teaching, distracts other students from learning, or disrupts their own learning. This broad definition of discipline surprises some folks, because it includes the passive, "reluctant" students who refuse to apply themselves to learning.

When students choose misbehavior over positive behavior, what do they hope to gain? Ultimately, they're seeking to belong, to find their place in the group. Along the way, however, they've become frustrated in trying to achieve the Three Cs in a positive manner, so they misbehave in an attempt to obtain immediate gratification. What they want usually corresponds to one of these four goals:

- attention
- power
- revenge
- avoidance-of-failure

Attention Some students choose misbehavior to get extra attention. They want to be center stage all the time, and constantly distract the teacher and classmates to gain an audience.

Power Some students misbehave in a quest for power. They want to be the boss—of themselves, the teacher, sometimes even the whole class. At the very least, they want to show others that "you can't push me around." They refuse to comply with classroom rules or teacher requests and often disrupt the established order.

Revenge Some students want to lash out to get even for real or imagined hurts. The target of the revenge may be the teacher, other students, or both.

We can help students find legitimate ways to satisfy their need to belong.

Avoidance-of-Failure Some students want to avoid repeated failure. They believe they can't live up to their own, their teachers', or their families' expectations. To compensate for this feeling of failure, they choose withdrawal behaviors that make them appear inadequate or disabled. Their hope is that everyone will back off and leave them alone so they won't have to be reminded that they aren't making the grade.

These four goals of misbehavior were first postulated in the 1930s by the noted educator Dr. Rudolf Dreikurs. When Dreikurs was asked why he had determined four goals instead of three, five, or eight, he reportedly responded, "I didn't make up these categories. I went out and observed children, and this is what I found."

If we carefully observe a student's misbehavior, we'll usually be able to identify its immediate goal as attention, power, revenge, or avoidance-of-failure. Admittedly, this sounds simplistic. Does every misbehavior really have one of these four goals? Of course not. No theory, no matter how complete, applies to every situation 100 percent of the time. Yet in my years of teaching, knowledge of the four goals has helped me classify about 90 percent of student misbehaviors. That's not a bad percentage. So until something better comes along, I'll stick with Dreikurs's theory.

Whether a student misbehaves for attention, power, or revenge, or to avoid failure, we're forced into responding; we have to interact with the student. If we're able to identify the goal of the misbehavior, we can interact effectively not only at once but also over time. Right away, we can redirect the misbehavior by using an intervention technique that suits the misbehavior. Over time, we can work toward eliminating further occurrences of the misbehavior by using encouragement techniques that build self-esteem. With time, the student will learn appropriate ways to feel capable, to connect, and to contribute. Thus, a little knowledge can give us a lot of advantage.

In our interactions with misbehaving students, we need to keep in mind that we can only *influence* their behavior. We can't change their behavior, for only they have this power of choice. But influencing such change becomes possible when we recognize that misbehavior is usually directed toward one of the four goals. The goals become our major clues in solving the misbehavior mystery. Once we're wise to what students are hoping to gain through misbehavior, we can help them find legitimate ways to satisfy their need to belong, ways that take their personal point of view into account. Consequently, we'll be on our way to creating a classroom environment that encourages appropriate behavior, fosters self-esteem, and motivates achievement.

Often those who need encouragement most are those we feel least like encouraging.

The "Difficult Child" Syndrome

Many educators talk about the "difficult child," the child for whom nothing in the typical repertoire of classroom strategies seems effective in reducing chronic misbehavior. I find the "difficult child" label counterproductive. The words themselves seem to indicate that something is inherently wrong with the child, as if being "difficult" is both the cause and explanation of the problem we're experiencing with this student. And by labeling these students "difficult," we subtly transform problem behavior into a personality trait. It's easy, then, to become discouraged and think that we can't help these students.

It makes much more sense to label behaviors, not students. The types of behavior that "difficult" children exhibit tend to be power and revenge behaviors, which are typically confrontive, often hostile, and definitely disruptive. To know how to intervene effectively, it's important to identify the goal of misbehavior using the categories of attention, power, revenge, and avoidance-of-failure. Different intervention strategies work with different goals. If we use the intervention strategies for attention seeking or avoidance-of-failure with power or revenge seekers, we won't get the results we're looking for. Instead of blaming students and labeling them "difficult," we need to change the way we handle the situation.

When students are unable to connect by behaving positively, they resort to misbehavior to achieve their goal.

In addition to intervention, these students often need huge doses of encouragement to influence them to satisfy their need to belong in positive rather than negative ways. The bind for teachers, however, is that these are precisely the students we feel least like encouraging. These students are often masters at manipulating adults. They have an uncanny way of spotting and magnifying our insecurities. Why should we have to spend our time and exert special efforts to encourage students who are repeatedly disrupting our classes and making our lives miserable? Shouldn't these students be expected to show at least some minor changes in their attitude and behavior before we modify ours?

If only it worked that way! Certainly it would be much fairer, since these students are the ones causing the problem in the first place. But, unfortunately, that's not the way of the world. We, the teachers, need to take the first steps. The good news is that, with hefty doses of encouragement and the use of appropriate techniques at the moment of misbehavior, teachers consistently report winning over most young people who previously had the label "difficult" attached to them.

The Truth Is in the Outcome

Hefty doses of encouragement and appropriate discipline techniques can win over many "difficult" students.

When I present workshops on Cooperative Discipline, teachers universally question the three basic concepts of behavior: "How do you know these concepts are true? You haven't provided scientific proof for them!"

My response is always the confession that no scientific proof justifies these principles. Theories about behavior are just that—theories. None is based on irrefutable scientific evidence. No one really knows the final and absolute truth about behavior.

Before you dismiss the concepts and this book, however, follow this suggestion and do what I do: *Pretend* that the concepts are true. *Pretend* that your students choose their behavior, that their ultimate need is to belong, that the goal of misbehavior can be categorized as attention, power, revenge, or avoidance-of-failure. If you adopt this attitude, I predict that you will experience positive changes in your classroom. Students who set your teeth on edge may become smiling and pleasant. Those who haven't done an honest day's work since the first day of school may become at least mildly enthusiastic about learning. Once you experience such changes, it won't matter whether the concepts are 100-percent true.

I've used these concepts of behavior in dealing with many students and with my own three children. Over the years, I've determined that they are the most effective ideas around. Until I'm convinced that other theories are more effective, I'll continue to believe in these concepts. I invite you to do the same.

CHAPTER 4
Characteristics of Attention-Seeking Behavior

Many misbehaving students are seeking extra attention. Note the term *extra*. We all need a certain amount of attention to feel that we're an important part of our social group. In contrast, students who misbehave for attention are never satisfied with a normal amount. They want more and more, as if they carry around with them a bucket labeled "Attention" that they expect the teacher to fill. There's a hole in the bucket, though, so no matter how much attention is put in, it seeps out. Since their bucket is never full, these students continue to misbehave.

The attention seeker's message is, "Look at me!"

Attention-seeking students are like stage performers: They require an audience. In the lower grades, the attention seekers usually gear their performance to the teacher. As these students move into the upper grades, especially middle and high school, they prefer a wider audience. They usually perform as much for their classmates as for their teachers. Some gain the notice of guidance counselors, administrators, and perhaps the entire school community.

Active Attention Seeking

Attention-seeking students are equipped with tricks I call AGMs— attention-getting mechanisms. For instance, Jackson, a second grader, has 101 AGMs. He taps his pencil on his desk, talks out of turn, trips classmates, wiggles his left ear while sticking out his tongue, and constantly pleads for help while his classmates quietly finish assignments. Jackson's sister Luci, a sophomore in high school, also has many AGMs. She regularly dashes into class ten minutes late, combs her hair in class, passes notes to friends across the room, loudly jangles her jewelry, and asks irrelevant questions during lectures.

Active AGMs are unmistakable. These misbehaviors disrupt the class and prevent us from teaching. If we don't take immediate corrective action, we risk losing control of the classroom.

Although the variety of AGMs is infinite, each type doesn't require a different response. Once Jackson's and Luci's teachers learn to deal effectively with attention-seeking behavior, the number and value of the two students' AGMs will gradually decrease.

Passive Attention Seeking

Passive attention-seeking students also employ AGMs. Unlike the active variety, however, passive AGMs rarely disrupt the entire class.

We may mistakenly think, "Thank heavens no one is misbehaving right now. I can proceed with today's lesson." We often fail to notice the passive attention seeker until the misbehavior gets under our skin. Or, we may ignore the behavior until we realize that the student's ability to learn has diminished or until we're able to find a moment to try to do something.

I like to describe passive AGMs as "one-pea-at-a-time" behavior. Did you ever watch a parent feeding a reluctant toddler? "Here, Penelope, eat one pea for Aunt Patty. Now take another for Uncle Pete. How about one for your brother Paul?" Three hours later, parent and child are still at the table, with seven more peas to go.

We see this one-pea-at-a-time behavior in students whose reaction time works only on slow, slower, and slowest speeds. These students are the dawdlers, the ones who haven't opened their math books when the rest of the class has already finished the third problem. We feel like shaking some life into them, although we know from observing them outside of the class that they really can move and react normally.

Redirecting passive AGMs is generally more difficult than redirecting active ones. Passive students often respond to attempts to get them moving by saying, "How come you're picking on me? I'm not bothering anybody." In contrast, the misbehavior of children who actively seek attention is so obvious that they can't deny their actions so easily.

How to Identify Attention-Seeking Behavior

Attention is a basic psychological need.

It's important to be able to identify attention-seeking behavior because different corrective strategies are effective with different goals of misbehavior. When a student misbehaves, therefore, we analyze a set of clues that make it fairly simple to distinguish among attention, power, revenge, and avoidance-of-failure behaviors.

The first clue comes when we take a reading on our "emotional pressure gauge" and note the nature and intensity of the feeling in the pit of our stomach at the moment of misbehavior. The second clue is evident as we become aware of how we typically react to this misbehavior. The third clue is the student response to our attempts to stop the misbehavior.

Attention Clue 1: When confronted with attention-seeking behavior, we generally feel *irritated and annoyed*. The needle on our emotional pressure gauge registers "mild."

Attention Clue 2: We typically react by nagging, reminding, cajoling, scolding—*using words* to try to discipline the child. Sometimes we react by *coming to the rescue*, taking over and doing for a student what the student should be doing independently.

Attention Clue 3: When we intervene verbally or by rescuing attention getters, they've gotten what they're looking for—our attention. So, *they usually stop* their negative behavior, at least temporarily. If they don't stop, chances are good we're dealing with power seeking rather than attention getting.

Origins of Attention-Seeking Behavior

How and why do children learn they can get more attention by misbehaving than by behaving? Two explanations are the "rewards" for misbehaving and that children haven't been taught to ask for attention in appropriate ways.

Rewards

Think about it: Parents and teachers almost always reward misbehavior with attention. The lesson begins in infancy. Babies cry, and parents come running. Babies amuse themselves happily, and parents tend to stay away, enjoying a rare moment of peace. As babies become toddlers, they learn that if they touch the controls on the TV or VCR, they receive immediate attention. But if they play contentedly with their blocks, they're usually ignored for a time. Childhood experiences like these reinforce the conclusion, "All I need to do to keep Mom and Dad busy with me is do something they've told me not to do." The attention gained is negative, but negative attention is far better than none at all.

Some bids for attention are less than subtle.

The desire for negative attention is also fostered unwittingly by teachers in everyday classroom situations:

> *T. R. is sitting quietly in the back row, completing geometry problems. Meanwhile, Jay is talking loudly to a girl across the aisle, disrupting at least a dozen classmates. Who does Mrs. Muñoz speak to? Jay, of course.*

Not Knowing How to Ask

Another circumstance that fosters attention-seeking behavior is the gap found in almost all our youths' education: No one teaches young people how to ask for attention in an appropriate manner when they believe they need it.

Just as food is a basic physical need, attention is a basic psychological need. We teach young people to recognize when they are physically hungry and to ask for food instead of simply wailing. Why not also teach them to recognize when they're psychologically hungry and to ask for attention? If we did this, students' need to misbehave for attention would diminish greatly. They might come into the classroom with requests such as these:

- "Mr. Burlingham, I'm feeling low and need a little extra attention today."
- "Could the class please give me one minute of undivided attention right now? I really need a boost this morning."

Contributing Factors

Most educators would agree that the number of students who misbehave for attention appears to be increasing. Is this because children receive less personal attention at home these days? Has the absence of extended family so deprived children of interpersonal contact outside school that they substitute attention from counselors and teachers? Perhaps too many hours spent in front of the TV or wandering around the mall contribute to the problem. As schools have grown larger and class sizes have increased, maybe students have discovered that the only way to get a reasonable amount of attention from school personnel is by misbehaving. Any or all of these factors may be contributing to the apparent increase in attention-seeking behavior.

Students' Legitimate Needs

When we closely examine attention-seeking behavior, we find some immediate needs that the student does not know how to satisfy appropriately. The student needs positive recognition—both verbal and nonverbal—that says, "I see you, I like you, and I'm glad that you're here today." Knowing this need is real helps us keep our emotions in check and be able to intervene at the moment of misbehavior in a calm, businesslike manner.

Positive recognition says, "I see you, I like you, and I'm glad that you're here today."

Attention-Seeking Behavior's Silver Lining

Attention-seeking behavior does have a silver lining. Students who seek a teacher's attention are at least showing they want a relationship with the teacher; they just don't know how to connect in a positive way. Most teachers would rather deal with a student demanding attention than with one who doesn't seem to care about anything or anyone.

If we recall this silver lining every time a student misbehaves for attention, our annoyance and irritation probably will diminish. By understanding the basic need to belong and recognizing that a child associates misbehavior with getting attention, we'll be able to take effective action.

Principles of Prevention

Two general principles can guide our efforts to prevent attention-seeking behavior in our classroom:

1. *Catch them being good.* Give lots of attention for appropriate behavior—two, three, even ten times more attention for positive behavior than for misbehavior.

2. *Teach them to ask for attention.* You can teach students to ask directly for extra attention when they think they need it. How would you like your students to ask for attention? What would you like them to say? One middle school has created "Notice Me, Please" cards that students simply hand to a teacher when they feel they need some positive recognition.

In later chapters we'll discuss how to apply both of these principles. For now, we'll go on to examine strategies we can use to intervene at the moment of attention-seeking behavior.

CHAPTER 5
When the Goal Is Attention: Interventions

*I*n this chapter, we'll explore many intervention techniques useful with students who choose to misbehave for attention. Choose first the techniques that make the most sense to you, fit your teaching style and personality, seem relatively easy to apply, and strike you as particularly appropriate for your students. Then try other techniques as needed. Most are easily adaptable for use at any grade level.

Strategy 1: Minimize the Attention

We walk a fine line when students misbehave for attention. Giving too much attention reinforces their mistaken notion that they belong only when they receive extra notice. On the other hand, we have to discourage such behavior when it disturbs our teaching and distracts other students from learning. A variety of attention-minimizing techniques can help us convince students to stop attention-seeking behavior without our reinforcing it.

Refuse to Respond Often, the best way to minimize attention-seeking behavior is to refuse to react to it. Our nonresponse wipes away the expected payoff.

When students misbehave for attention, we can ask ourselves: What would happen if I ignored the behavior instead of interfering? If the answer is that the attention seeker would be inconvenienced and no one else would be affected, ignoring the misbehavior is likely to be effective. When students don't receive the anticipated attention, they'll usually abandon their efforts after a few tries.

Give "The Eye" "Stare them down," recommends a savvy seventh-grade teacher. "They know what they're doing, they know you know what they're doing, and they know that 'The Eye' means 'Stop.'" With this technique the teacher doesn't use words—just looks. Eye contact is the only attention students receive.

Stand Close By Physical proximity is another tool that helps minimize attention-seeking behavior. While continuing with the lesson, the teacher simply moves to stand next to the misbehaving student. No eye contact is made, and nothing is said. The student's efforts will usually be discouraged when the teacher's presence is so immediate.

I CAN'T TALK NOW— MR. J. IS GIVING ME "THE EYE."

Eye contact can do a lot to discourage irritating behavior.

Use Name Dropping This technique gives minimum recognition to the misbehavior while communicating that the student should stop the behavior and attend to the lesson. The teacher periodically inserts the student's name into the context of the lesson: "Now during this period—Melissa—in American history—Melissa—the settlers journeyed—Melissa . . ." This technique also can be used in conjunction with The Eye or with standing next to the student.

Send a General Signal For years, teachers have used signals to help students realize that their behavior choice at the moment is inappropriate. For example, many students have been taught that a teacher's upheld hand with two fingers raised or crossed means "Stop what you're doing and pay attention to me." Similarly, a finger placed perpendicular to closed lips means "Silence—now." We can easily establish other similar signals to use when a number of students are off-task and seeking attention. Because many students today come from cultures where such signals are not in general use (or have different meanings), we need to teach the meaning of every signal we use.

Physical proximity is a tool that helps minimize attention-seeking behavior.

One clever teacher establishes the "Give Me Five" routine early in the year. The five fingers of the right hand each have a different meaning: hands quiet, pencils down, mouths closed, sit still, eyes on the teacher. When things are beginning to get out of hand, she says in a fairly loud voice, "Give me five!" Then she starts counting down one finger at a time.

A different variation of a general signal is used by a resource teacher:

She teaches her students a few words in sign language: yes, no, sit, stop, good, listen, and time to go. She uses these signs, as necessary, while continuing to teach. Intrigued with the signs, students now use them to signal one another. For example, when a student is doing seatwork and a classmate begins to interrupt, the student simply signals "No."

Send a Secret Signal A modification of the general signal is to establish a secret signal with one student. Consider my experience with Barry, a second grader who interrupted me during lessons:

One day, in desperation, I asked Barry, "What do I have to do to keep you quiet while I'm busy with other children?" Barry responded by making a motion with his hands as though he were squeezing an imaginary basketball. "What does that mean?" I asked him. "It means 'Get it together,'" Barry replied.

Then and there, Barry and I made an agreement that whenever I gave him that squeeze signal, he would stop what he was doing and get back to work. Believe it or not, the signal worked! I'd often add a wink when making the sign. Barry would smile and settle down, satisfied that he'd had two seconds of my time just for him. For years afterward, whenever he'd pass me in the hall or on the playground, Barry would make our secret signal. That I'd cared enough to share the signal with him continued to make our relationship special.

Signals can also be verbal. One middle school music teacher experienced success with a budding musician who would frequently speak out inappropriately during orchestra practice:

During a very short one-on-one conference, the teacher and student together decided that the secret signal would be saying the name of a composer. The test of the signal came the next day when the student interrupted practice. The teacher calmly looked at her music and said, "Beethoven." The student immediately became quiet while the rest of the class looked puzzled, wondering what they'd missed.

Give Written Notice Since we know that tomorrow we'll be faced with students misbehaving for attention, we can prepare today by duplicating a stack of notes that give this message: "Please stop what you are doing right now." When students interrupt for attention, we can just drop one of these notes on their desk. We don't need to utter a word—the note says it all. This technique works particularly well with high schoolers.

Use an I-Message There are times when we just want to say "Stop!" to a student who is disrupting the classroom. Psychologists tell us that the most effective way to do this is to deliver an *I-message*: "Cornelia, when you talk to your neighbor during class discussions, I get annoyed because I lose my train of thought. Please stop."

Notice the four parts to the I-message:

1. It contains an objective description of the disruptive behavior: *"When you talk to your neighbor . . ."*
2. It relates our feeling: *"I get annoyed . . ."*
3. It identifies the effect of the misbehavior on us or on the class: *". . . because I lose my train of thought."*
4. It finishes with a request: *"Please stop."*

I-messages tell students exactly how we feel. With attention seekers, talking about our feelings in this brief, nonpersonal way isn't a payoff for misbehavior. I-messages are particularly effective with adolescents because they are clearly understandable, businesslike, and mutually respectful.

I-messages tell students exactly how we feel without judging or blaming.

Strategy 2: Clarify Desired Behavior

Students misbehaving for attention often lose focus and forget what they're supposed to be doing. We can refocus them in a couple of ways.

State "Grandma's Law" The basis of Grandma's Law is the axiom "First we work, then we play." We first state the behavior *we* want, then give permission to do something *they* want to do afterward:

- "When you finish outlining the causes of the Civil War, then you may use the computer."
- "When today's word problems are completed, then you may choose an enrichment activity in the lab."

Notice that Grandma's Law always follows a "when-then" format. Avoid using an "if-then" format instead. Students who have the penchant for escalating attention-seeking behaviors into full-blown power struggles are prone to interpreting "if" statements as threats. These students love to test us to see if we'll carry through on what we've said.

Use "Target-Stop-Do" Being direct and forceful in stating a desired behavior is especially effective with students who have auditory or attention-deficit problems. This three-part message, given in a calm, matter-of-fact tone of voice, *targets* the student by name, identifies the behavior to be *stopped*, and tells the student what he or she is expected to *do* at that moment:

- "Luciano, stop talking to Ben, face me, and see if you can find a solution to problem 3 on the board."
- "Damita, stop drawing, open your workbook, and finish page 24."

One reason Grandma's Law and Target-Stop-Do statements are effective is that both techniques state the specific desired actions in behavioral terms. We leave no doubt in the student's mind as to what is expected. Another reason is that they replace the familiar teacher lecture that begins, "How many times do I have to tell you . . . ?" Instead, they simply give the factual information students need to choose more appropriate behavior.

Strategy 3: Legitimize the Behavior

Like Pandora and her box, many students find it hard to resist doing what they're told not to do. We can take away the fun from this type of misbehavior by using techniques that legitimize it.

Create a Lesson From the Misbehavior Here's an example that a junior high teacher shared with me:

The students in Mr. Hardy's science class seemed to be obsessed with spitballs. None of the usual methods for banishing spitballs worked, so Mr. Hardy decided to legitimize the behavior. He told the class that he was going to teach an entire unit on spitballs. He had students plot trajectories, conduct time and distance studies, and keep copious notes on their experiments. By the time the three-week unit was finished, the students wanted nothing more to do with spitballs!

Most students are quick to stop a misbehavior when it is legitimized and turned into "work" by the teacher.

And here's how one middle school teacher dealt with a seventh grader who intentionally farted in class:

He gave the student the assignment of researching the definition of the word flatulence, *along with writing a report on the medical procedure for examining people who had bowel difficulties. It wasn't long before this student cured himself of his offensive habit.*

Go the Distance When we go the distance, we extend a behavior to its most extreme form. One way to do this is to ask the students to perform the misbehavior ad infinitum. Here's how an art teacher reports applying this technique:

In my art class that meets before lunch, I had three eighth-grade boys who'd picked up on the term putty knife *in wood shop earlier in the day. They decided to say these words randomly throughout art class, ignoring my polite request to stop. When the lunch bell rang, I kept the boys after class. I told them to stay in the room for three minutes and continuously say their phrase, "Putty knife." I closed the door, attended to my hall duties, and listened through the door as they repeated their by now not-so-wonderful phrase. After three minutes I opened the door and dismissed them to lunch. The group effort was never repeated.*

Going the distance is effective with many similar harmless yet annoying behaviors. For instance, students who don't stay in their seats can be requested to stand for the entire period. Students who talk constantly can be required to fill an hour-long audiocassette with their words.

It's important to keep remembering that different interventions work with different goals of misbehavior. Had the three boys in art class been into power behaviors, there's no way the teacher could have *made* them keep repeating their "putty knife" phrase.

Have the Class Join In Simon is tapping his pencil on his desk—again. "Okay, class," you announce. "Pick up your pencils and tap them for the next two minutes." With everyone participating in the misbehavior, Simon loses his payoff: He's not getting special attention from anyone. Since pencil tapping has become legitimate, the fun has vanished.

Using this technique may cost some minutes of teaching time. Remember, though, that whenever we're interrupted by an annoying behavior, we also lose teaching time. Isn't it better to do something likely to end a misbehavior than to spend precious minutes repeatedly trying to correct it?

Use a Diminishing Quota This technique was first recommended by Dr. Rudolf Dreikurs.[1] It involves allowing incidents of particular misbehaviors to occur, but only in the number agreed on beforehand and with the stipulation that the number will decrease daily. Consider how Kai's teacher might use this technique to convince him to choose different behavior:

> *Kai burps loudly at least a dozen times during each civics class. One morning, in a private conversation with Kai, his teacher negotiates how many burps will be allowed in class that day. Each time Kai burps, his teacher just smiles at him and makes a slash mark in the corner of the chalkboard. When Kai reaches his quota for the day, the teacher shrugs and gestures "That's it" to him. The teacher and Kai continue negotiating a lower number each day until the behavior disappears.*

You may be thinking, "Wait a minute. What if the student goes over the quota?" If that happens, abandon this technique and substitute another, or analyze the misbehavior again to see if its goal might actually be power. The technique of using a diminishing quota works only with attention-seeking behaviors.

Teachers who've used this technique report that most students adhere to the quota. Why? Because the private conversation, the smiles, and the slash marks provide all the needed attention. The students are not in a power struggle with their teachers—they just want that bit of attention that makes them feel they belong.

A quick laugh relieves tension and refreshes the atmosphere.

Strategy 4: Do the Unexpected

Frequently, we can end attention-seeking behavior by doing the unexpected. By using this strategy, we give this message: "I see you and know what you are doing, but I'm not going to play your game." Since the game of misbehavior requires at least two players, it's just about over when the teacher withdraws.

The more humor we can use when doing the unexpected, the better. Garrison Keillor says, "Humor is a presence in the world—like grace—and shines on everybody." The more humor can shine in our classroom at the moment of misbehavior, the more quickly and easily the moment will pass.

Turn Out the Lights Teachers have used this old standby for years. When a student (or an entire class) gets out of hand, simply flick off the lights and wait silently for a few moments. There's no need to give Lecture 385 on what the students are doing wrong; they know when they're misbehaving. In this situation, silence speaks louder than words.

Play a Musical Sound Music teachers and primary teachers often play a chord or a progression of chords on the piano at the moment of misbehavior. If there's no piano handy, we can use any kind of instrument that appeals to us—a bell, cymbals, a tambourine.

Lower Your Voice Yelling when students misbehave adds another dimension to the confusion already in the classroom. At the same time, it reduces the students' sense of belonging and self-esteem. When we lower our voice, however, students have to pay attention and strain to hear us. This distracts them from misbehaving. When we talk quietly, they talk quietly, creating a productive classroom atmosphere for all.

Change Your Voice Use unusual speech patterns or sounds—even gibberish. Chant or sing words, talk in a monotone, speak in a high or low pitch, or mix the two. Any of these vocal changes will distract students misbehaving for attention.

One word of caution, though: Don't mimic real speech patterns, accents, or languages. Though we may not intend it, mimicking can hurt or offend.

Some teachers find a secret signal to be effective.

Talk to the Wall This technique was reported to me by a middle school teacher:

> When one or more of her students misbehave for attention, she walks over to a wall and begins a monologue: "Oh, Wall, you wouldn't believe what is happening in my room just now. Someone is calling out without raising her hand. Someone else is tipping back on his chair. Will you just look at the student who is passing a note in the back of the room? Please, Wall, don't just stand there. Help me with this bunch of kids."

If you decide to try this technique, you might want to warn your principal in advance that you talk to walls. Otherwise, the principal may decide you're a candidate for a mental health leave!

Use One-Liners Any quick quip will distract the misbehaving student, as long as it's uttered in fun, without a hint of sarcasm. One fourth-grade teacher has a magic vacuum cleaner. As an immediate response to a misbehavior, he often says, "Wait a minute. Here comes my magic vacuum cleaner to suck you up." And even tenth graders responded to their English teacher's dramatic one-liner: "To be or not to be—cooperative!"

Cease Teaching Temporarily Students know we're in school to teach. When we interrupt a lesson to "do nothing" for a few minutes, we send students a powerful message to change their behavior. Three variations of this technique work effectively with attention-seeking behavior, especially when several students are acting irresponsibly at the same time.

1. *Give a nonverbal message.* Simply stand and silently scan the room, with a matter-of-fact facial expression. The message you are sending is: "What I have to say is important enough for everyone to be listening." Once the class is paying attention, begin teaching immediately. Avoid the temptation to make the students "suffer" in silence or to deliver a lecture on wasted class time.

2. *Sit down on the job.* Use this variation when students are so caught up in what they're doing that they do not notice you are no longer teaching. Sit down in front of the class, fold your hands, and continue to scan the room with the same matter-of-fact look.

3. *Pick up the book.* Make your seated message even more obvious by picking up your *Cooperative Discipline* book and starting to read it silently. This is particularly helpful if you're having difficulty maintaining a blasé expression—you can always cover your face with the book! When you have the students' full attention, put the book down; stand and deliver.

Strategy 5: Distract the Student

No one can do two things at once for very long. Therefore, we can distract students from continuing inappropriate behavior by focusing their attention elsewhere.

Ask a Direct Question The moment of misbehavior is a fine time to ask the student a direct question:

- "Justin, what are the instructions I just gave?"
- "Nenka, how would you tackle this physics problem?"

Questions like these not only distract students from their misbehavior but also focus their attention on the lesson at hand. For extra emphasis, combine this technique with one of the minimizing techniques discussed for Strategy 1.

Ask a Favor This is another time-honored way to redirect students who seek attention:

- "Gina, please collect everyone's essay."
- "Khan, would you mind taking the attendance sheet to the office right now?"
- "Josh, please go to Ms. Gargin's room and ask if she could loan us the CD-ROM on the human body."

If this technique is used too often, smart students might begin viewing the request of a favor as their reward for misbehaving. Used occasionally, however, it works just fine.

Give Choices Students love choices. Choices give them a sense of control over their lives, turning their attention away from attention-seeking behavior and toward making the choice. The choices we offer need not be anything momentous. Appropriate choices often center on *which, how, where,* or *when:*

- "LaToya, you may do any three of the six physics problems on the board. You decide."
- "Marty, you may complete this assignment at your desk, at the social studies activity center, or in the study center in the back of the room. Which location do you prefer?"
- "Maureen, you may present your report Tuesday or Thursday. Which do you choose?"

Change the Activity If many students are misbehaving simultaneously in a bid for attention, a change of activity usually distracts them from this misbehavior. Ask them to clear their desks, listen to new instructions, or take out different books.

Strategy 6: Notice Appropriate Behavior

Rather than speak directly to a student who is misbehaving, we can say something positive to someone who is sitting near the student and behaving appropriately. In this way, we convey the message that good behavior, not misbehavior, receives the payoff.

Many students will be satisfied with only two seconds of our time just for them.

Use Proximity Praise We can thank a student who is doing just what we want the misbehaving student to be doing:

- "Thank you, Juanita, for having your algebra book open to the correct page and your eyes focused on the board."
- "Thanks, Evan, for keeping your hands to yourself and your feet under your chair."

Such statements relay exactly what behavior is expected of the misbehaving student.

This technique works best if we describe the desired behavior in objective terms. General statements such as "Juanita, thanks for being so good" or "Thanks, Evan, for doing what you're supposed to do" are not as effective because they don't clearly communicate our expectations. And be careful to avoid thanking the same students too often, or they'll be set up as teacher's pets and resented by their classmates.

In the elementary grades, proximity praise can be said aloud. As students get older, however, we're more successful when we're discreet, standing nearby and toning down our volume so that only the students involved hear what we have to say. Thanking a small group works equally well—especially with older students.

Use Compliance Praise When proximity praise has the desired effect on the misbehaving student, take a moment to thank that student for choosing to cooperate. This little bit of positive attention can be a powerful positive reinforcer. Again, be discreet with secondary students—a private statement works best. Speak just loud enough so a few neighbors can hear.

Make Recordings We can write the names of those students who are behaving appropriately on the chalkboard, on a clipboard, or on a file card. This not only reinforces desirable behavior but also sends a subtle message to misbehaving students to stop. An additional benefit is that we're developing a class culture that appreciates positive behavior rather than the put-downs and negativity that all too often become the focus of student attention.

Give a Standing Ovation Break up the routine, add a little movement and fun to the class, and redirect a misbehaving student at the same time by announcing:

- "Let's have a standing ovation for everyone who is looking at page 77 of the social studies book."
- "Let's stand up and applaud for all the students who are listening quietly to the directions."

After a minute or two of clapping and hooting and hollering, most students are willing to settle down and finish the task at hand, putting away their AGMs at least for the moment.

Strategy 7: Move the Student

Most attention seekers like to have an audience. When we remove such students from their audience, we're taking away some of their reward, which inclines them to end the misbehavior. Two techniques are effective for accomplishing this.

Change the Student's Seat Sometimes a change of seat is all that's needed: "Willie, please move to the empty seat in the third row." Continue the lesson while Willie moves, so he doesn't receive any undue class attention. Even though such attention would be embarrassing, Willie still might consider it a reward for his misbehavior.

Use the Thinking Chair Some teachers place a "thinking chair" in a quiet area of the room, out of the direct line of vision between the teacher and the rest of the class. The thinking chair in my classroom was an old wicker chair that I'd picked up at a flea market and painted purple. Any chair that's handy will do, as long as it doesn't resemble the other chairs in the classroom.

The purpose of this chair is to provide a spot where misbehaving students can think about how they will act differently when they return to their seats. Five minutes in the chair is generally enough time—even less for primary students. The rest of the class should understand that someone in the thinking chair is never to be disturbed.

All we need to say to a misbehaving student is, "Molly, please go sit in the thinking chair." If Molly doesn't move quietly to the chair, she may be seeking power rather than attention. Likewise, if she misbehaves again when her time in the chair is up, her goal is probably power. A different intervention technique is then necessary.

Note

1. Rudolf Dreikurs, *Psychology in the Classroom* (New York: Harper and Row, 1957, 1968), 141-42.

Dealing With Attention-Seeking Behavior

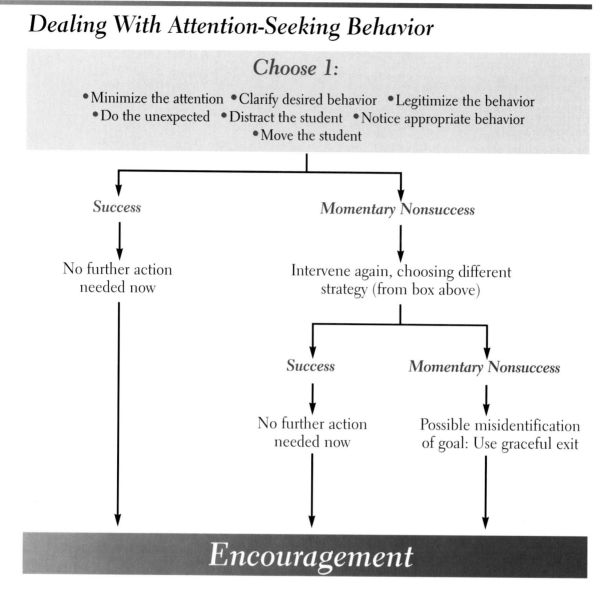

Choose 1:

• Minimize the attention • Clarify desired behavior • Legitimize the behavior
• Do the unexpected • Distract the student • Notice appropriate behavior
• Move the student

Success

No further action
needed now

Momentary Nonsuccess

Intervene again, choosing different
strategy (from box above)

Success

No further action
needed now

Momentary Nonsuccess

Possible misidentification
of goal: Use graceful exit

Encouragement

Assumptions
1. Intervention used correctly
2. Guidelines for avoiding and defusing confrontations
   (Chapter 8) followed

Power-seeking students constantly challenge us. Through words and actions, they try to prove that they, not we, are in charge. Sometimes they stage a scene over major issues such as incomplete work or making noise while others are working. At other times they challenge us over relatively insignificant issues such as muttering under their breath or chewing gum in phys. ed. They may completely disregard our instructions, comply insolently, or use colorful language as a challenge to our authority.

Often power-seeking students don't act out until they're assured of an audience. We fear that if we lose such a public battle, we'll be permanently labeled a "loser" by the entire class. The pressure of having to handle a difficult situation with so much at stake in front of an audience adds greatly to our discomfort.

Power behaviors, like attention-seeking behaviors, display both active and passive modes. Let's consider the active mode first, since it's easier to notice.

Active Power Seeking

Tantrums are the most obvious form of power-seeking behavior.

Young people don't lose their temper; they use it. Primary students, from preschool through the first couple of grades, may demonstrate temper by crying, kicking, rolling on the floor, and refusing to listen.

Older students tend to throw verbal tantrums, often termed "lip" or "sass." They talk back to the teacher in a disrespectful, defiant manner: "You can't make me write out that chemistry experiment. Mr. Gunderman doesn't make his class do all that extra stuff, so I'm not going to do it either." Power-hungry students know more than a million variations on the you-can't-make-me-do-it theme.

One variation of verbal tantrums is the "lawyer syndrome." Students who use this behavior are bright and fluent. Instead of acting disrespectfully, they speak in a pleasant manner while using pseudo-logic to explain misbehavior: "There's no sense in my writing out that chemistry experiment because it takes away from the time I could better spend memorizing formulas. You saw me perform the experiment in class, so you already know that I can do it correctly."

One variation on verbal tantrums is the "lawyer syndrome."

The first time we lock horns with lawyer-syndrome students, we might be impressed by their verbal acuity. Repeated encounters wear us out, however, and we quickly become disenchanted with their linguistic acrobatics.

Passive Power Seeking

Passive power seekers have a variety of quiet, but effective, ways to challenge their teachers.

Quiet Noncompliance

Passive power seekers rarely cause a scene, because they've noticed that their classmates often get into double trouble for a single incident of misbehavior—once for not complying and once for spouting off at the mouth when confronted. Passive power seekers therefore avoid the pitched battle. Instead, they smile at us and say what we want to hear. They then do precisely what they want to do. Mali's actions exemplify this behavior:

> *Mr. Rubeyov passed out the writing assignment ten minutes ago, and Mali is still staring out the window, blank paper on her desk. "Is anything wrong?" Mr. Rubeyov asks her. Mali smiles and shakes her head. "Why is your paper blank?" he then inquires. "I'm thinking," Mali replies. Next he asks tentatively, "Do you plan to complete the assignment?" She nods yes. At the end of the period Mr. Rubeyov collects the papers; Mali's paper remains blank.*

Mali has defied Mr. Rubeyov as clearly as if she'd said, "I won't do it." She has done so, however, in such a way that he may not recognize that a power struggle is occurring. Having become caught up in Mali's words, which sound compliant, it has taken a while for the teacher to realize that Mali's actions are a direct challenge to his authority.

When we are faced with a similar situation, we should first ascertain that our teaching methods and materials are appropriate for the student. We should also ensure that no learning disability or skill deficiencies could account for the student's actions. Once this has been done, we can be fairly certain that the motivation for such behavior is passive power.

Students seeking passive power exhibit sneaky behavior, for their words represent one thing and their actions another. When we receive such mixed messages from students, we tend to believe the words, not the behavior. So when a student says "I will" and then proves by subsequent actions "I won't," we keep hoping that somehow the "I will" is going to win out in the end. It won't—not until we respond differently.

The power seeker's message is, "Let's fight."

Why do we tend to believe the words and not the behavior? Perhaps because teachers tend to be verbal people. Words, after all, are our business. We may also be idealistic and want to give students the benefit of the doubt: "If Mali says she'll do it, I keep hoping she will." Perhaps we believe the words because believing the behavior would demand corrective action, and we're not sure what action to take.

Hiding Behind a Label

If we recall what psychologists have been maintaining for a long time—that it's far easier to lie with words than with behavior—then we'll quickly realize that the words of passive power seekers constitute a lie. When Mali says "I'm working on it" and then turns in a blank paper, she has, in effect, lied. But *lie* is a loaded word, with all kinds of unpleasant ramifications. Since it's risky to call anyone a liar, teachers and students use all kinds of euphemistic terms or labels to justify the discrepancy between what passive power seekers say they will do and what they actually do.

Unfortunately, these labels may interfere with our taking appropriate disciplinary action. A label transforms a bid for power, which is really misbehavior, into an ingrained personality trait that the student couldn't possibly be expected to overcome. We may use labels to explain to parents and administrators why we're not having success redirecting a student. Moreover, once we've labeled the student, we can more or less ignore the student and concentrate instead on coping with those engaged in more disruptive behavior.

Passive power seekers tell us what we want to hear. Then they do what they want.

The Lazy Label Alexia comes in on Monday morning without her weekend assignment. She smiles apologetically and says, "I'm sorry I didn't get it done. I really meant to do it, but I guess I'm just too lazy. I'll try to do better next time—really."

Alexia's contrition will win an extension from many teachers. After all, her good intentions should count for something. If she had told the truth instead—"I just didn't feel like doing homework this weekend"—she would have risked her teacher's wrath and might have faced unpleasant consequences.

Laziness is a cover-up, an excuse for slacking off. It is a chosen behavior, and once we have identified it as power-seeking behavior in operation, we can work to change it.

The Forgetful Label "Oh, I forgot to do it!" is a phrase the average teacher hears thousands of times. Saying "I forgot" is more acceptable than saying "I refuse." No one has ever been suspended from school for forgetting!

Occasionally, the "forgetful" excuse is appropriate, as when some neurological condition causes a student to forget things unintentionally. And we all experience a memory lapse from time to time. The distinction is that unintentional forgetting happens across the board—

pleasant things as well as unpleasant things are forgotten. In contrast, power-seeking forgetfulness happens only when something unpleasant is supposed to be done, such as chores or homework. The same student who invariably forgets homework assignments can probably recite with ease which TV programs are broadcast on Monday night or the phone numbers of five friends.

The Short-Attention-Span Label

A short attention span is another trait that a few young people neurologically have and that a large number exploit. The exploiters find that exhibiting a short attention span is a convenient way to get teachers off their back and reduce their workload.

Take the case of Theo, a first grader who can't seem to concentrate on whatever the class is doing. His attention wanders, his body wanders, and his poor teacher has to wander after him. Yet during free time, Theo sits and builds elaborately in the block corner for nearly an hour, never moving his little bottom one inch. Suddenly, his attention span is just fine!

As in the case of forgetting, if the student is selective with a short attention span, be suspicious. The problem could very well be a "choosing disability" rather than a learning disability.

The Underachieving Label

A few years ago I counseled a student labeled an "underachiever" by his teachers:

Although he was gifted intellectually, his grades were poor and his work habits nonexistent. Despite an unimpressive high school record, he used his charm to persuade a nearby state university to accept him.

During his first college vacation, he told me that he'd received an A in physics. When I asked if he'd been getting As all along in physics, he said that he'd flunked the first three exams. When I expressed surprise that he'd been able to turn things around so well, he grinned and said, "It was easy. I just figured out that all I had to do was study."

My head spun with the thought of how many times over the past years this young man's teachers had pleaded with him to study. This student's underachieving had been his way of exhibiting passive power all along. Fortunately, he realized on his own that he had the ability to change his behavior.

Many times I've had students explain to me why they chose to do just so much work and no more in a specific class. In their own minds, they were reaching their goals precisely. This passive power behavior tells the teacher, "I'll decide exactly what level to achieve. You can't make that decision for me."

The Listening-Problems Label Sometimes students who use passivity to gain power are said to have listening problems. If a student shows evidence of a real hearing problem, by all means have an audiologist run some tests. But many students with "listening problems" hear what we say perfectly well; they just choose not to respond in the way we want them to.

Other Labels Other labels used for passive power behaviors include "strong willed," "stubborn," "unmotivated," "apathetic," and "oppositionally defiant." Of course, students who refuse to do work are stubborn, and students who won't follow rules are indeed strong willed. No genetic basis exists for such behavior—though some parents will argue this point: "I know Brianna is giving you trouble in class, but she's just like her father, the most stubborn person on earth. I guess we'll just have to live with it."

No, we don't have to live with it! Once we help students see that they *do* have the ability to change their behavior, we can influence them to make more responsible choices.

Some students learn to exploit the short-attention-span label.

Distinguishing Disabilities From Passive Power Seeking

Distinguishing a real learning disability from passive power behavior is not easy. A key tip-off is selectivity. If the student fails to perform only when asked to do something but seems capable of completing tasks he or she selects independently, we can be fairly sure that we're dealing with a passive bid for power.

Some students may confuse us further by combining a small, legitimate disability with a large chunk of power behavior:

> *Craig is a ninth grader who has a slight auditory retention problem. If he looks directly at the teacher during lectures so that visual cues are combined with auditory cues, and if he takes copious notes, Craig can retain most information. When he chooses not to work, however, he consistently pleads, "I don't remember hearing that." Craig's problem is not with listening but rather with doing; he uses his slight disability as a cover-up for choosing not to do what needs to be done.*

Whenever we suspect that a student may have a disability, we need to work with support staff to find the exact nature of the problem. Once we know a student's capabilities, we can expect the student to live up to potential, and we can treat any slacking off for what it is: passive power-seeking behavior.

How to Identify Power-Seeking Behavior

We know that the goal of misbehavior can be for attention, power, revenge, or avoidance-of-failure. It's important to be able to identify the goal at the moment of misbehavior to know how to intervene effectively. Different intervention strategies work with different goals.

Earlier, we discussed three clues for distinguishing attention, power, revenge, and avoidance-of-failure goals: Our emotional pressure gauge, our reaction, and the student's response.

Power Clue 1: When we find ourselves in a power struggle, our emotional pressure gauge rises to a reading of "hot." We feel *angry*, *frustrated*, and perhaps even *fearful of losing control* of the situation—and of the class.

Power Clue 2: One typical impulsive reaction in a power struggle is our attempt to regain control by *fighting back with words*. Should our emotions get the best of us, we might find ourselves making sarcastic, humiliating, esteem-crushing remarks—words that we're sorry for as soon as they leave our lips. Unfortunately, when we fight with words and use our status to overpower the student, we risk escalating the goal to revenge, with the student vowing to get even with us later.

Another typical impulsive reaction is simply to *give in*: "What's the use?" we rhetorically ask ourselves. "We've been down this route before and nothing works with this kid." Teachers who use the hands-off style of discipline often throw up their hands in this manner.

Power Clue 3: The last clue for identifying power behavior lies in the student's response to correction. Power behavior doesn't stop as quickly or as easily as attention-seeking behavior. After all, students who seek power are trying to show us that they're the boss and that they'll do things their way. So the misbehavior doesn't stop until somehow it's made to look like it has stopped—on the student's terms, not ours.

Power-hungry students make three responses in an attempt to show us who's in charge. Sometimes *they respond to correction on slow speed*. They do what we ask them to do, but slowly, taking an inordinate amount of time to perform the simplest task. Students know how much their slow response irks us, how anxious we are to end the confrontation and return to our teaching.

A second frustrating student response to correction during a power struggle is to *repeat the behavior one more time*. We say "Stop rocking the desk." They rock it one more time, grin, and then let it rest.

A third exasperating response is to *mumble under their breath*, just loud enough for us to know they're muttering but not to hear the exact words.

It's important to identify the goal of power at the moment of misbehavior.

Origins of Power-Seeking Behavior

Unfortunately, power-seeking behavior is on the rise. Hundreds of teachers corroborate this wherever I go. Teachers also are seeing more of this behavior with younger students. Even preschools and kindergartens are increasingly filled with children who want to be the boss and do everything their way.

Changes in Relationships

The growth of power behavior in the classroom is a reflection of rapid changes occurring in the world around us. One hundred years ago, power relationships in our society were clearly defined. Dad ruled the household; Mom and the kids complied. Bosses ruled the workplace, and workers who challenged them lost their jobs. Teachers were governed by school boards that dictated everything from lifestyle to moral code.

Within this pecking order, children were at the bottom. They were to be seen and not heard, and any use of power tactics on their part led to severe punishment. In a time when students could see the dominant-submissive relationship at work all around them, they accepted (though not necessarily liked) the "rule of the paddle."

Today all that has changed. No class or group of people accepts a subservient role. Everyone demands equality. Women seek equal rights, equal pay, equal responsibilities. Workers form unions, insist on a voice in wage settlements and working conditions. Teachers, no longer willing to accept the "benevolent wisdom" of school boards, speak up about what they want, need, and will do.

The quest for personal power is pervasive. Young people notice this and want what they consider their fair piece of the action. In a society where almost no one models unconditional compliance with authority, we can't expect students to assume a subservient attitude. The only way to convince them to reaccept the rule of the paddle would be to provide them with suitable models of the dominant-subservient relationship. Women, workers, and even teachers would have to be persuaded to return to the roles of an earlier day.

I admit to having oversimplified a complex historical process, but the fact is that power relationships in society have been irrevocably altered. We can't turn back the clock; we can only move forward with the times. As teachers, we have to learn new strategies for coping with a relatively new and increasingly prevalent kind of classroom behavior.

The Human Potential Movement

The rise of power behavior has been hastened in the last few decades by a second factor: the trend toward personal growth and development. This trend is epitomized by the human potential movement that

> *The quest for personal power is pervasive. Young people notice this and want what they consider their fair piece of the action.*

began in the late 1960s. The focus of the movement was the exaltation of the individual and the gain of personal power. People read books and attended workshops with themes such as "Unleashing Personal Power." For many, involvement in this movement has been a positive experience.

In response to the personal growth trend, educators developed affective education. Their duty became not only to teach students the traditional three Rs but also to help them define their personal values, develop their individual talents, and enhance their social skills. For young people—as for the adults involved in the human potential movement—affective education has generally been a positive experience.

Young people, however, sometimes confuse personal power with a desire for *interpersonal* power. When this happens, they may overstep the bounds and attempt to control not only themselves but also their teachers and classmates. As a result, teachers have to learn how to sidestep the power struggles and help students exercise legitimate personal power in ways that enhance the classroom atmosphere while satisfying student individuality.

Students' Legitimate Needs

When we closely examine power-seeking behavior, we find some immediate needs that students do not know how to satisfy with appropriate behavior. Students, especially those in middle and high schools, need freedom to feel and be in charge of themselves and their lives, to be able to make decisions based on what they think is best for them. This need for autonomy is related to adolescents' developmental need to put distance between themselves and their parents. Acknowledging this need, to ourselves and even to the students, helps us keep our perspective—and our cool—when faced with a power-driven student.

Power-Seeking Behavior's Silver Lining

Like attention-seeking behavior, power-seeking behavior has a silver lining. Many students who engage in this behavior—especially the active, verbal variety—exhibit desirable personal characteristics such as leadership potential, assertiveness, and independent thinking. These students will never be human doormats. By wanting to think for themselves and control their own lives, they exhibit the signs of what represents good mental health in adults.

If we are able to keep this silver lining in mind, we will be more able to appreciate students' legitimate bids for power and deal constructively with those that are misguided.

Principles of Prevention

We can think of students who engage us in power confrontations as dangling a fishhook in front of us. Their challenging words are the bait. They're itching for us to bite and argue back. If we refuse to bite at the hook the first time it's thrown at us, they change the bait and dangle the hook in front of us again . . . and again . . . and again.

Three principles of prevention for power-seeking behavior influence students to leave their fishing poles at home:

1. *Allow voice and choice.* To many students, having their *say* is as important as having their *way*. What they want most is for us to listen to their concerns and ideas. When we can respond to their ideas by giving them a choice of options, they know they've been heard and that we're on their side.

2. *Grant legitimate power.* When we implement a hands-joined management style and involve students in the decision-making process, we are giving them the legitimate power that helps prevent power struggles.

3. *Delegate responsibility.* Students who have a sense of real responsibility are less likely to strive for power in destructive ways.

In Chapter 9, we'll look at a variety of strategies we can use to intervene during power confrontations.

To many students, having their say *is as important as having their* way.

CHAPTER 7
Characteristics of Revenge-Seeking Behavior

Young people who seek attention or power can be delightful, charming students when not misbehaving. Not so students who habitually seek revenge. These students often sulk and scowl even when not lashing out. They put us on edge because they seem ready to explode at the slightest provocation. Their cumulative folders, full of adjectives such as *mean*, *vicious*, and *violent*, warn that trouble lies ahead.

When students misbehave to get revenge, they are retaliating for real or imagined hurts. Such behavior often follows power-seeking tactics, especially if the teacher has responded to the power behavior with a show of force. Although we are able to put students back in their place for a moment with a show of our own power, doing so is usually counterproductive, for it spawns worse misbehavior as students seek revenge. The misbehavior may come two minutes, two hours, two days, or two weeks after the original confrontation, but we can bet it's coming! Although we may win the battle by force, we'll lose the war by siege.

Not all revenge behavior results from a power struggle with a teacher. Sometimes the revenge seeker feels slighted by the teacher, even though the slight is unintentional. I encountered such a situation with Randy, one of my second graders:

Randy frequently declared how much he disliked me. This hurt my feelings, since I liked him and went out of my way to be nice to him. One day, he decided to attack me indirectly by "accidentally" knocking over a plant. That was the last straw for me. "What have I done to make you dislike me so much?" I demanded. His eyes full of hurt, Randy replied, "How come I never get to take the erasers outside? You don't like me as much as the other kids!"

I was stunned by Randy's interpretation of events. I never dreamed that clapping the erasers outside was considered such a treat. I thought it was a great bore and assigned it to students at random. Once I was able to understand things from Randy's perspective, I knew why he acted as he did and was able to end the revenge attacks.

Revengeful students may not be angry with their teacher. They may feel they have been hurt by parents, other teachers, administrators, or peers—people against whom revenge might be too risky. The teacher then becomes a handy scapegoat, available five days a week. Teachers may also become ready targets when young people experience anger or hurt because of a distressing personal circumstance such as divorce, parental unemployment, or racial prejudice.

Students who use the verbal variety of revenge know 1,001 ways to say "I hate you."

Active Revenge Seeking

Active revenge-seeking behavior takes many forms. It may be direct or indirect, physical or psychological.

Direct Physical Attacks

In keeping with the ever-increasing violence of the times, students frequently threaten teachers with bodily harm. From elbow jabs to knife slashings to aiming loaded guns, violent student behavior is no longer merely a teacher's nightmare but a frighteningly real possibility.

Indirect Physical Attacks

Students get indirect physical revenge by breaking, damaging, or stealing something. Angry students may knock breakable items off our desk, snip buds off our plants, let air out of our tires, or take money from our wallet. Since students know we care about school property, they may break classroom windows, smash computer monitors, rip pages out of library books, or spray-paint lavatory walls.

Revenge seekers always know which words will hurt most.

Psychological Attacks

Equally alarming to teachers are the psychological "games" to which revenge seekers challenge us.

Verbal Variety Verbal psychological attacks frequently assume the form of threats, insults, or criticisms. Students who use this tactic know 1,001 ways to say "I hate you." Such psychological attacks rarely reflect the true quality of the teacher-student relationship. Rather, they are meant to manipulate the teacher into feeling hurt and guilty.

Here are some of the most common varieties of psychological attack:

- "You're the worst teacher I've had yet."
- "My sister sure is lucky. She has a great teacher this year."
- "I'm glad I don't really need to know this subject to get into college because I sure can't learn anything in this class."
- "If this class was any more boring, they'd have to give out pillows with the books."

If we recognize such statements as revenge-seeking behavior, we won't get caught up in endless verbal battles, trying to convince students to change their minds.

Action Variety Students usually know what values teachers hold dear. A favorite way to seek psychological revenge is to violate these values. For example, if we believe that cleanliness is next to godliness, students who want to hurt us may keep their desks in disarray or turn in sloppily done assignments. If students know we value politeness, they may attempt to irk us by shoving other students in the hall or by swearing in class. If we insist on punctuality, revengeful students may appear three minutes late to class and turn in all assignments one day late. In short, students frequently find the right button to push when they want to get a rise out of teachers.

Some extreme revenge actions may hurt students as much as or more than teachers and parents. Unfortunately, some students want revenge so badly that they are willing to hurt themselves to get it. Rebellious delinquency, pregnancy, excessive eating or dieting, and drug abuse are transgressions of adult values that almost always have negative consequences for students. Suicide, sad to say, is the ultimate form of revenge for a few severely discouraged young people.

The revenge seeker's message is, "I'll get even!"

Passive Revenge Seeking

Most revenge behaviors are active, not passive. The hurtful messages come through loud and clear. The only revenge behavior that could be classified as passive is withdrawal. Withdrawn students are sullen, uncommunicative, and remote. We reach out to them in every way we know, but they consistently turn away. Their lack of response is meant to hurt and frustrate us, and it does. After all, we're teachers— we want to help, and we take pride in being able to make contact with students. Students get their revenge: We dance rings around them trying unsuccessfully to elicit a response but end up feeling guilty, worn out, and wounded by constant rejection.

How to Identify Revenge-Seeking Behavior

Different intervention strategies work with different goals. For this reason, it's important that we be able to recognize a goal of revenge at the moment of the misbehavior. We've learned three clues for distinguishing attention, power, revenge, and avoidance-of-failure goals: Our emotional pressure gauge, our reaction, and the student's response.

Revenge Clue 1: Our emotional pressure gauge reads "mild" for attention and "hot" for power. With revenge behavior, the needle jumps to "boiling." We not only *feel anger and frustration,* but *hurt, disappointment, and even dislike* for the student.

Students who make passive bids for revenge seek to hurt and frustrate us.

Revenge Clue 2: One typical impulsive reaction when faced with revenge behavior is to *want to strike back* by saying and doing something hurtful in retaliation. Another is to *punish severely*, assuming a "You can't get away with this" posture. A third impulsive reaction is to *withdraw* from the student, avoiding as much contact as possible. If your instinct at the moment of misbehavior is to react in any of these ways, you have a clue that you are dealing with revenge behavior.

Revenge Clue 3: The last clue for identifying revenge behavior lies in the student's response to correction. Revenge behavior doesn't stop as quickly or as easily as attention getting. As with power struggles, revenge behavior continues until it somehow appears to have stopped on the student's terms. The difference here between revenge and power, however, is that students seeking revenge usually *intensify the misbehavior* in some way before they decide to stop. They do or say something particularly damaging or hurtful—to our possessions, our psyches, or the class.

Origins of Revenge-Seeking Behavior

Like power seeking, revenge behavior in schools is on the rise. Some of the major contributing factors are the increasing violence in society and the pervasive sense that material goods and economic opportunities are unfairly distributed.

Violence Is Everywhere

Everywhere, crime is growing. TV and movie screens are filled with acts of violence. So are city streets, country roads, and suburban sidewalks. And, in our ever-faster-paced world, many young people feel a sense of frustration and powerlessness. Rarely do children see hurt feelings or anger expressed in positive ways. Instead, they constantly observe people lashing out at one another, with words and with weapons. It's not surprising, then, that their own feelings boil into similarly uncontrolled violence.

Students' Legitimate Needs

When we closely examine revenge-seeking behavior, we find some immediate needs that students do not know how to satisfy appropriately. Students who seek revenge are hurting inside. They see and live with poverty, unemployment, racism, divorce, abuse, crime-ridden neighborhoods, and a growing sense of powerlessness and inequality. This list of ugly happenings in the lives of all too many students goes on and on. The world is not safe—physically or psychologically—for this generation of youth.

Young people have a legitimate need for safety and security, to grow up knowing they are cared for and protected until they are mature enough to make it on their own. The lack of safety and security can lead to the angry, hostile emotions that we see acted out in the classroom.

Revenge-Seeking Behavior's Silver Lining

To see the silver lining in revenge behavior, we have to switch our perspective to that of the students. They see the hurting of another person as a means of protecting themselves from further hurt. They actually are showing a spark of life in their actions. For the sake of their own mental health, they're better off doing something than doing nothing. A student who feels hurt but does nothing about it is likely to be overcome by feelings of hopelessness and despair. Such feelings, if they last long enough and are strong enough, can lead to chronic depression, even suicide. Suppressed feelings of pain are not the only cause of teenage suicide, of course, but they constitute a major contributing factor.

Principles of Prevention

Two general principles are applicable for preventing or decreasing the amount of revenge behavior occurring in our classroom:

1. **Build caring relationships.** Reassuring students that we care about them despite their actions takes a great deal of courage and commitment. It's natural to resent a person who wants to hurt us. However, if we can manage to "separate the deed from the doer," as Chaim Ginott admonishes,[1] we'll be more willing to implement the encouragement strategies that clearly demonstrate to students that—despite their unacceptable behavior—we do care for them.

We can teach students how to express their hurt and hostility appropriately.

2. *Teach appropriate expression of feelings.* We can teach students how to express their hurt and hostility appropriately and invite them to talk to us when they are upset. When students learn such skills, they learn how to cope with intense feelings by negotiating and communicating rather than lashing out.

In Chapter 10 we will look in more detail at ways we can put these prevention principles into practice.

Note

1. Chaim G. Ginott, *Teacher and Child: A Book for Parents and Teachers* (New York: Avon Books, 1972), 71.

CHAPTER 8
Avoiding and Defusing Confrontations

This chapter is a prelude to looking at specific interventions for power and revenge. It presents guidelines that are most helpful in applying intervention strategies for those two goals. The guidelines here concern *us*: how *we* should behave when our students misbehave. By following the guidelines, we can shape our attitudes and actions to achieve the desired outcome of a teacher-student interaction. No matter how well we've matched an intervention to a misbehavior, we risk sabotaging success if our attitudes and actions are inappropriate.

Guideline 1: Focus on the Behavior, Not the Student

When we intervene to stop a misbehavior, we want to describe misbehavior objectively. Chaim Ginott said it clearly: "Focus on the deed, not the doer; on the behavior, not the student."[1]

Describe Behavior—Don't Evaluate When talking with students about their misbehavior, we need to use objective terms. If we concentrate on telling Tonye exactly what she is doing to cause us grief, we can avoid slipping in subjective terms such as *bad*, *wrong*, or *stupid*. Subjective terms provoke negative emotional reactions in the student (and us) and get in the way of solutions.

Deal With the Moment When using an intervention technique, we need to deal only with what is happening at the moment. References to the past or to the future lock both the student and us into thinking that the misbehavior is part of an unalterable pattern. After all, if Abe "always" behaves in a certain way, and if we predict that he "always will," why should he try to behave differently?

Be Firm and Friendly We need to be *firm* toward the misbehavior, thus making it clear that it must stop. At the same time, we need to be *friendly* toward the student, thereby communicating our continuing care and interest. A firm-but-friendly[2] posture says to the student, "What you are doing must stop right now, but I still like you." This attitude of acceptance projects our belief that the student is capable of behavior that's appropriate. That belief can become a self-fulfilling prophecy.

References to the past or future lock the student and us into thinking the misbehavior is part of an unalterable pattern.

Guideline 2: Take Charge of Negative Emotions[3]

When a student misbehaves—particularly for power or revenge—our emotional response is immediately negative. We may feel angry, frustrated, fearful, or devastated. To feel such emotions is normal. To act them out, however, is counterproductive.

Control Negative Emotions When we allow anger to choke us or frustration to overwhelm us, we can't think clearly or act logically. Worse, our display of such negative emotions may reinforce the student's decision to misbehave. Our anger is part of the desired payoff for students seeking power or revenge. Thus, when we show them our anger, we're encouraging them to continue the misbehavior. A young person who can upset a grown-up is powerful indeed! Elementary, middle, and high schoolers all enjoy a sense of power when they know they've succeeded in flustering a teacher.

Dealing with misbehavior is like being forced to play a game. The student always starts the game by doing something unacceptable and then waiting for us to make a predictable move—generally to react emotionally. When we take charge of our emotions and respond in a reasoned, noncombative manner, we "check," or block, the student's strategy and thus communicate that we're unwilling to play the game. This gives us and the student the opportunity to become teammates trying to solve a mutual problem rather than opponents trying to outwit one another.

Release Negative Emotions After we've responded to a misbehavior that's really upset us, we often have a lot of leftover negative feelings. To get through the remainder of the teaching day without developing a headache or ulcers, we can promise ourselves that we'll get rid of the emotions as soon as we're in an environment where it's appropriate to do so. When we know relief is coming, we're usually able to contain our emotions for as long as necessary, without jeopardizing our interactions with students.

Many of us can find relief through physical outlets. A brisk walk after school can help release negative emotions. For the more athletic among us, so can jogging, running, or playing tennis. Those more practical might be surprised at how swiftly yardwork or housework can be accomplished when emotional energy is put into it!

My personal preference for releasing negative emotions is a verbal outlet. The audience is composed of me, and the environment is my car. On the way home from school, I keep the car windows closed, turn on the air-conditioning or heater so no other drivers can hear me, and pretend that the student I'm angry with is seated beside me. Then I let go with everything I'd like to say to the student.

If you want to try my method of releasing emotions, temporarily forget about the concepts that we've established for dealing with misbehavior. You don't have to focus on the behavior, be logical, or even maintain coherence. Just let it pour out, unrehearsed and unedited. Nothing you say can harm anyone. Be as loud as you want, and use whatever language you wish. I guarantee that by the time you reach your destination, you'll feel calmer than when you began the journey.

Guideline 3: Avoid Escalating the Situation

This recommendation goes hand in hand with the previous guideline. At the moment of misbehavior, we need to avoid certain behaviors that will only make the situation worse for both the student and us. To obtain a sampling of advice on what we should try to avoid doing or saying, I've surveyed scores of teachers, asking what specific behaviors have backfired for them. Here are some of their responses:

A student who can cause a grown-up to become unglued is powerful indeed.

raising my voice
yelling
saying "I'm the boss here"
insisting on the last word
using tense body language
    (rigid posture, clenched
    hands)
using degrading or
    embarrassing put-downs
using sarcasm or humiliation
attacking the student's
    character
acting superior
using physical force
drawing unrelated persons
    into the conflict
having a double standard
    ("Do as I say, not as I do")
insisting I'm right
preaching

making assumptions
backing the student into a
    corner
pleading or bribing
bringing up unrelated events
generalizing about students
    ("All you _____s are the
    same")
making unsubstantiated
    accusations
holding a grudge
nagging
throwing a temper tantrum
mimicking the student
making comparisons with
    siblings, other students
commanding, demanding,
    dominating
rewarding the student

Some of these behaviors may stop a student from misbehaving—for the moment. But we'll pay too high a price for this short period of control. Eventually, the negative side effects of our own behavior will give us more trouble than the student's original misbehavior. We risk propelling students into a more difficult interaction with the teacher, from attention-seeking into power behavior or from power into revenge behavior.

All of the behaviors hinder students from feeling that essential sense of belonging. Most also reduce students' self-esteem. Why risk such negative side effects when we have the option of choosing more effective behaviors!

Were you surprised to discover *rewarding* on the list? Too often, rewards encourage students to misbehave again in hopes of receiving more benefits. In addition, rewards promote a bargaining mentality in some students. If we offer Tom a reward of ten minutes' extra free time if he'll stop dawdling and finish his language worksheet, tomorrow he may ask, "If I finish this, do I get ten minutes of free time again?" If we say no, the worksheet probably will be completed s-l-o-w-l-y. If we say yes, we may soon hear Tom demand, "Teacher, I want fifteen minutes of free time for doing this math sheet." Before long, Leah may ask, "If I finish, do I get extra free time too?" Soon our classroom will sound like *Let's Make a Deal,* and we can forget about inspiring learning for its own sake.

Guideline 4: Discuss Misbehavior Later

There is a proper time for talking about misbehavior and negotiating solutions. That time, however, is rarely at the moment of misbehavior. A brief, direct, firm, and friendly intervention is the best bet at the moment. Save the discussion for later.

Talk about misbehavior later — when everyone has calmed down.

Why not discuss misbehavior when it happens? Because neither teacher nor student will be able to hear the other's words; the moment is too emotional for both. This is particularly true of power and revenge confrontations, during which feelings run especially high.

The time to talk about the misbehavior is later—when everyone has calmed down and can respond rationally. This may be an hour later; it may be tomorrow. By then we'll be able to describe the misbehavior for the student in ways that focus on the act, not the actor. We'll also be able to explain more clearly the effects and consequences of the misbehavior.

How will students know that their behavior is wrong if we don't tell them so at the moment? The answer to this legitimate concern is that most young people know what constitutes misbehavior and what the effects of that misbehavior will be. Consider Darryl, a seventh grader who shouts out four-letter words during health class. Does Darryl need to be told that his behavior is unacceptable? Not at all. In fact, we only increase his payoff if we stop class to give Lecture 527 on the evils of profanity. Better to intervene immediately, saving the discussion for a time when Darryl's not getting the glory of it.

Students won't think we're condoning the misbehavior of their classmates if we hold general discussions about misbehavior from time to time. During these discussions, they'll learn what's acceptable and what's not. In addition, they'll learn that we will intervene quickly when someone misbehaves.

Guideline 5: Allow Students to Save Face

Students who seek power feel important only when they appear to be running the show. In their hearts, though, they know that the teacher has the ultimate authority and that they'll have to choose appropriate behavior eventually. As a result, they often try to play a game with us called "My Way." In this game, they give us what we want but stamp their compliance with a small gesture that says, "Okay, I'll do it—but *my* way, not yours." If we go along, we allow them to save face, and they give us what we want. Both players win.

A common ploy in the game of "My Way" is muttering. We ask tenth-grader Riata to stop walking around the room and to return to her seat. She complies, but as she sits down, she mutters something under her breath. Her voice is not loud enough for us to understand what she's saying. If we decide that Riata needs to sit down our way, not her way, the scene may proceed like this:

Teacher: Riata, what did you say?
Riata: (very softly) Nothing.
Teacher: I heard you, Riata. I want you to tell me what you said.
Riata: (in a loud, sarcastic voice) I was only thinking out loud. Are you against thinking?

By insisting that students do things our way, we risk provoking a new confrontation, one that is often more unpleasant than the original. Is it worth it?

We also need to realize that a student's reaction to correction, such as muttering, is usually a normal human reaction—not a vindictive personal attack. For example, consider what the reaction might be in the following situation:

You're sitting in an emergency faculty meeting convened by your principal at 3:30 P.M. The principal has just distributed five inventory supply forms, saying that all the forms must be filled out immediately.

What happens next? The room probably becomes filled with muttering, a perfectly human reaction when we're asked to do something we'd rather not do. Knowing that we must comply, we let off steam by muttering.

By insisting that students do things our way, we risk provoking a new confrontation.

The game of "My Way" includes other tactics besides muttering. Students may take a few more seconds than necessary to comply or make a face or gesture of displeasure. They may repeat the forbidden action one last time before stopping or say something rude to have the last word. Allowing students to save face in these relatively harmless ways usually stops the misbehavior fairly quickly. Everyone's need has been met: The teacher has achieved compliance, and the student has retained pride. Everybody wins!

Notes

1. Chaim G. Ginott, *Teacher and Child: A Book for Parents and Teachers* (New York: Avon Books, 1972), 71.
2. This was a favorite aphorism of Dr. Rudolf Dreikurs.
3. Technically speaking, emotions are neither "negative" nor "positive." They are what they are. In popular usage, however, the feelings discussed—anger, hurt, frustration, hopelessness—are generally considered negative. So for ease of communication, I'll occasionally refer to "negative emotions."

Chapter 9
When the Goal Is Power or Revenge: Interventions

No aspect of discipline is more difficult than dealing with power and revenge behaviors. The confrontations and disruptions that accompany them exhaust us, waste valuable teaching time, and dissipate our dedication.

Power and revenge behaviors can be compared to the eruption of a volcano. A volcano begins with the rumbling stage, during which the earth shakes and steam begins to spout forth. Next comes the mighty explosion, which destroys everything in its path. Eventually the resolution stage is reached, in which we cope with the damage and take steps to prevent further destruction.

Like the volcano, power and revenge confrontations begin at the rumbling stage, with students using annoying antics to tempt us into a confrontation. Once we're hooked, the explosion comes—unpleasant words and behaviors spurt forth. Eventually, we reach the resolution stage, when we try to get everyone back to normal and prevent future confrontations.

Three Stages of a Classroom Volcano

This chapter presents intervention techniques for dealing with each stage of a classroom volcano. The techniques are grouped under three general strategies that correspond to the stages:

- The Rumbling Stage: Make a Graceful Exit
- The Eruption Stage: Use Time-Out
- The Resolution Stage: Set Consequences
                  Conduct a Teacher-Student Conference

If a graceful exit technique is successful at the rumbling stage, the eruption stage may be avoided. But despite our best efforts and no matter how polished our skills, the confrontation might reach the eruption stage. When this happens, we use a time-out technique, which enables both us and the student to calm down before entering the resolution stage. At the resolution stage, we implement techniques that hold students accountable for their misbehavior and educate them to make more appropriate choices in the future.

Emergency Preparedness

There's no escaping classroom volcanoes—no matter how well we teach, implement prevention principles, or encourage students. Sooner or later every teacher will hear the rumbling and perhaps even the roar of an exploding volcano. Knowing volcanoes are "natural occurrences," we can take steps to be prepared and to minimize the fallout.

Remain Unimpressed At the moment of confrontation, students want our full attention. How powerful they feel when they get a rise out of us! If we get so upset that our behavior becomes worse than theirs, they feel justified in continuing the misbehavior. Reminding ourselves of how they're trying to manipulate the situation helps us keep our cool. The more indifferent we are to the hot lava spewing forth, the smaller the payoff for students' disruptive behavior. Remaining unimpressed shows that we're in control of ourselves and of the situation.

Use Mental Reminders When our authority is challenged by power-seeking students, however, remaining unimpressed isn't easy. As a classroom teacher, you will find it helpful to keep your cool at these moments by giving yourself these reminders:

Mental reminders help teachers stay cool, calm, and in control.

- "The only person I have control over is me."
- "I can control my personal reaction to what's happening."
- "I am a good teacher. Just because _____ is exploding right now doesn't change that fact."
- "I can handle this situation. It's not so awful. I only have to decide which graceful exit I want to use right now."
- "Students will know I'm in control if I remain calm."

Then quickly scan the room. Seeing that the majority of students are staying calm and cooperative will help you keep things in perspective despite the volcano in your midst.

Check the Barometer Meeting and greeting students at the door as they enter the classroom serves many purposes. For students who typically exhibit power and revenge behaviors, these few moments allow us to take their pressure readings. When we detect a rumbling volcano, we can ask a favor, give a choice, suggest the student spend a few minutes with a counselor or dean before entering the classroom, or use encouragement to prevent the volcano from erupting.

Keep Your Black Belt Handy No, not for striking the student! This black belt refers to the Japanese art of *aikido*. The mind-set of aikido is to go with the flow rather than fight back or retreat. A master of aikido pivots when attacked, deflecting the force of the attacker's motion and remaining in control of the situation. A master of "teacher aikido" uses verbal pivots called graceful exits.

The Rumbling Stage: Make a Graceful Exit

At the rumbling stage, we're warned that a full-scale confrontation is coming. We might see the warning in students' faces or body language, or hear it in their voices. We might sense it when they smile and disregard our instructions or ignore school rules. The warning gives us a chance to sidestep the confrontation by using a graceful exit. This technique is a diplomatic maneuver that allows all involved to save face. No one emerges as a winner or a loser; everyone is given the opportunity to escape a heated situation.

When making a graceful exit, we need to remain as calm as possible. Any sarcasm or animosity in our voice or actions will provoke a further challenge. The more humor we can bring to the situation, the more graceful the exit for all concerned. Humor, however, should be directed toward the teacher or the situation—never the student. A remark that is embarrassing or humiliating only escalates the situation.

Acknowledge Students' Power

That teachers have the power to *make* students do things is an illusion. For example, suppose Dawn refuses to do her math assignments. We can threaten and cajole, take away rights and privileges, and send notes home until we're blue in the face. But if Dawn doesn't *choose* to do the work, it won't get done. The more we try to control the student, the more the student resists.

Instead of fighting this losing battle, we can acknowledge the student's power: "Dawn, I can't *make* you do the math problems." When we give up control, the student has nothing to resist. Does this mean that we relinquish all authority? That students like Dawn get to do whatever they want? Absolutely not. Once the student's resistance has been lowered and the confrontation calmed, we can use a consequence to influence Dawn to choose more appropriate behavior. People who feel dominated often react by resisting the person in charge. When we acknowledge that we can't dominate, we admit the student's equal status as a human being. When students see that no one in the classroom is superior or inferior, we gain their cooperation rather than fuel confrontation.

Our relaxed body language and calm tone of voice convey to students that we're in charge of ourselves and the situation.

When you acknowledge a student's power, you can also state your expectation: "Dawn, I can't *make* you do the math problems. But the assignment needs to be completed." As soon as you've said this, walk away. It's hard to continue a war of words when the opponent is no longer nearby.

That teachers have the power to make students do things is an illusion.

Remove the Audience

Dr. Oscar Christensen of the University of Arizona loves to tell this story about power interaction:

> *The two tall gladiators were having a real go of it in front of a crowd of students gathered outside the lunchroom. I walked up, told them to stop immediately, and was totally ignored. So then I said, "Anyone caught standing in this hall in one minute will be put on detention." The crowd dispersed immediately. A minute later, the gladiators noticed that their audience had deserted them, and stopped dead in their tracks. At that point I was able to remove the gladiators to my office to settle the matter between them in a more peaceful manner.*

When others are standing by to see who wins, confrontations invariably intensify. On the other hand, performances are usually pointless without spectators to applaud. In the classroom, sending the audience somewhere else is rarely possible. Removing the audience's *attention*, however, can be equally effective.

There are many ways to do this. You can make an important announcement. Or, initiate a discussion on a topic of general interest. Change the activity. Do something unexpected. Anything that distracts the rest of the class removes the audience—and a major part of the payoff—from the disruptive student. Again, walk as far away from the misbehaving student as possible. Remember, distance makes it difficult for the student to continue the verbal fight.

We can sometimes postpone a classroom confrontation until the period has ended or until a transition time when students will leave or move around the room. For example: "Carter, we'll finish discussing this matter as soon as the bell rings." Once class is over and Carter is without an audience, he may lose interest in a confrontation.

Table the Matter

It's the last class of the day, and we're weary to the bone. Hannah chooses this moment to challenge us by telling her friend—and the class at large—just how stupid she thinks last night's assignment was. All eyes are on us, awaiting our next move. If we tangle with Hannah, the whole class is likely to get out of control, and we'll probably end up with a first-class headache.

As teachers, our best way out of such situations is to use a simple sentence or two that postpones resolution of the issue until we're better able to cope. We can choose our own time and place to continue the discussion, when the audience is gone and we're less emotional. Here are some examples of statements that can effectively table discussion:

- "I'm not willing to talk with you about this right now."
- "Would you rather fight or solve this problem?" If a student chooses "fight" we reply, "But not with me. Who would you like to fight about it with? The principal? Your parents?"
- "You may be right. Let's talk about it later."

Another way to table the matter is to place a "gripe box" in the classroom. Ask the student who confronts you to write down the complaint and place it in the gripe box. Use the written note as the starting point for a conference or a class discussion or meeting at a later time. Make sure to establish guidelines when introducing the gripe box so that students don't abuse the privilege with profanity and put-downs.

In the classroom, sending the audience somewhere else is rarely possible.

Schedule a Conference

Keep a clipboard handy with a note that says "Please choose the time you prefer for a conference with me" and lists times you are available for private conversation. When a student begins to challenge you, silently hand the clipboard to the student and walk away. Pick up the clipboard at the end of the class period. If the student has not signed up, select the conference time yourself and state the time you will expect the student to come talk.

When in our busy schedules do we have time to conference with students? Homeroom. Lunch. Recess. Between classes. During planning periods. Before and after school. When the rest of the class is doing independent work, small-group work, or a cooperative learning activity. Depending upon the behavior, conferences can be as short as two minutes or as long as fifteen.

Use a Fogging Technique

When students attack us verbally, our best strategy is to use a fogging technique. This involves responding to inflammatory statements as if they are of little or no importance. Such a response tells students that we cannot be manipulated by insults.

Fogging techniques may seem contradictory to the skill of active listening, which acknowledges the importance of what students are saying. When students are verbally attacking us, however, active listening will only prolong the confrontation. If the misbehaving students really wanted to discuss something, they'd bring up the matter at a more appropriate time and place. If necessary, use the clipboard-conference technique to set a time to listen to and discuss a student's feelings.

Agree With the Student

Agree With the Student This is one of the most effective fogging techniques. When students make insulting statements, the last response they expect from us is agreement. When we agree, students have no way to continue the confrontation.

> *Luis sneeringly informs Ms. Hickory that she's by far the worst teacher on the planet. Ms. Hickory responds simply, "You may be right. Now open your Contemporary Lit book to page fifty-seven." If Luis continues to insult Ms. Hickory, she can continue to agree cheerfully while calmly reminding him which page the class is working on. After a short time, Luis will realize that he does not have the power to engage Ms. Hickory in a confrontation she does not choose to join, and he will drop his challenge.*

Change the Subject

Change the Subject If we reply to verbal attacks by changing the subject, we can deflate the student's challenge.

> *Ms. Hickory might respond to Luis's insult by asking him if he watched the football game last night. If his attack continues, she can respond with a comment on the weather or tell a joke. Like a broken record, she can repeat her lines over and over again until Luis gets the message that she's not going to fight.*

We aren't condoning a student's words when we don't reply directly to an attack. The student knows that the words are inappropriate and hurtful. A lecture on "Why Students Should Respect Teachers" won't help either; it will only prolong the confrontation. Our goal is to get the student to end the misbehavior. If we can accomplish this quickly through fogging, we aren't required to do anything else at the moment.

State Both Viewpoints

State Both Viewpoints The first half of this simple two-part statement uses *reflective listening* to let the student know that he or she has been heard. The second half states the teacher's position on the issue at hand. The format for stating both viewpoints is "To you _____. To me _____."

- "*To you* a written report on the hole in the ozone layer seems a waste of time. *To me* it's an important ecological problem that warrants your attention."
- "*To you* it seems foolish to have to walk in the halls. *To me* it's a safety rule that must be followed."
- "*To you* it seems like I'm being unfair when I lower grades for assignments turned in after the due date. *To me* it's a logical consequence for not meeting an important deadline."

Should the student continue to argue, make the distinction between understanding and agreeing. Demanding that students agree with our point of view will just prolong the power struggle because they'll perceive agreement as "losing." Asking for understanding, however, lets the student save face and see the outcome of the situation as a draw.

Refuse Responsibility

Students often initiate power struggles with statements such as "I can't do it because _____." For every logical explanation we give they find another rebuttal. Instead, refuse responsibility with a positive statement: "I'm sure you can figure it out." A word of caution: Double-check your identification of the goal of misbehavior before using this technique. If the goal is avoidance-of-failure, the student will be further discouraged if you refuse responsibility, when in reality help is needed.

Agreeing can be an excellent fogging technique.

Dodge Irrelevant Issues

We've all had students throw irrelevant issues at us in the middle of a power struggle, hoping to throw us off balance. For example, after first refusing to complete the history assignment on the board, Rosa says, "You just don't like kids who live in my neighborhood." We don't need to take part in a socioeconomic debate. A simple response of "That's not the issue. The issue is _____" puts us back in control of the situation.

Dodge "I don't agree" declarations too. Responses such as "I'm not asking you to agree. I simply want to know if you understand the issue" allow both teacher and student to exit gracefully. Should the student attempt to continue the debate at this point, switch strategies and use the clipboard-conference technique described earlier in this chapter.

Deliver a Closing Statement

Closing statements are one-liners that communicate to the student that for us the confrontation has ended. As with all of the graceful exit techniques, we need to be especially careful that our manner is calm and our tone of voice neutral. No sarcasm allowed. Some examples of closing statements include:

- "Are you done yet?"
- "You've mistaken me for someone who wants to fight."
- "You're confusing me with someone else. I don't argue with students."
- "Unless you have something new to add, I'm finished with this conversation."

Call the Student's Bluff

This technique always begins with the phrase "Let me get this straight." It clarifies the position the student is taking: "Let me get this straight. I asked you to _____ and you are refusing. Is this correct?"

The choice is to choose more appropriate behavior immediately or be held accountable for continual disruption. Some teachers stand with a notebook or audiocassette player, ready to record the student's response to the question. When teachers call a student's bluff in this respectful, businesslike way, the student is put on the spot. Knowing that their exact words may be reported to an administrator or a parent, students often end the confrontation.

Take Teacher Time-Out If you find yourself losing your cool, you can extract yourself from the situation with a teacher time-out. Make a simple pronouncement such as:

- "What's happening right now is not okay with me. I need some teacher time-out to think about it. We'll talk later."
- "I need some time to get control of my thoughts. Give me a few minutes, please."
- "I'm calling time-out. I need a few minutes to calm down."
- "I'm going to walk away now and give myself some time to chill out. We'll talk later."

Teacher time-out allows both teacher and student to save face, regroup, and resolve the situation at a later, less emotional time. This technique also affords us the opportunity to model for students that when we are losing control we can ask for time-out to "get it together."

The Eruption Stage: Use Time-Out

For some students, sitting on a chair while phones ring and teachers buzz by is much too rewarding.

If a confrontation can't be contained during the rumbling stage, look out! The explosion is coming! Once we've entered the eruption stage, we'd be wise to get out of the way—fast. The various time-out techniques can help us do just that. Time-out involves isolating the student from the rest of the class. The frequency and seriousness of the misbehavior determines where we send the student. The time-out techniques are presented here in order of increasing severity.

Occasionally, revenge encounters bypass the rumbling stage and begin with the eruption. This can occur if the student has been upset by something that happened elsewhere—at home, in another classroom, on the playground. Once the explosion happens, we have to deal with the here and now and can't worry about where and why the behavior originated.

Time-Out in the Classroom A time-out area for young children in a self-contained classroom should be out of the direct line of vision of the rest of the students. One way to create such a space is to partition off a small area of the room with a piano, bookcase, or movable chalkboard or bulletin board.

Time-Out in Another Classroom

An effective time-out area could be another classroom of the same grade. The students in another classroom usually aren't interested in being an audience for someone from a different room, so they probably will ignore the misbehaving student. When the payoff of peer attention is removed, the student is less likely to continue the misbehavior.

I don't recommend sending a student to a classroom of younger children, since this move will likely embarrass or humiliate the student. A child whose self-esteem is thus lowered is not likely to be convinced to choose appropriate behavior. However, sending a student to a class of older children to experience how more mature students behave is acceptable.

Once we've entered the eruption stage, it's too late for a graceful exit.

Time-Out in a Special Room

As a step between another classroom and the principal's office, some schools set up a supervised time-out area, detention room, or in-school suspension area to isolate misbehaving students from classmates.

Time-Out in the Office

The principal's office should be used only as a last resort. For some students, sitting on a chair while phones ring and teachers buzz by is much too rewarding. Besides, why advertise that our student has gotten so out of hand? Despite the disadvantages, though, we may have to use the office when all other in-school choices have failed or the misbehavior is so malicious that intermediate steps are out of the question.

Time-Out in the Home

The most severe time-out technique is suspension from school. This step should be avoided whenever possible since often no adult is home during the day to supervise a student who has been suspended. Many young people consider staying out of school a reward, not a punishment.

Implementing Time-Out

Some students will stubbornly refuse to go to a time-out area. Two techniques give teachers an effective way to set and enforce limits to disruptive behaviors in this situation: using *language of choice* or calling on the *who squad.*

Language of Choice

When we tell confrontive students what they "must do right now," we are asking for further resistance. Often giving a choice is more effective: "Bonita, you may sit quietly in your seat without bothering others, or you may go chill out in Mr. Jordan's room. You decide." If Bonita verbally agrees to behave appropriately but continues to misbehave, the teacher can say, "I see by your behavior that you have chosen to go to Mr. Jordan's room. Please go now." No second chances. It's time for action, not words.

The language of choice usually defuses confrontations because we are not commanding or threatening. We simply state the specific behavior expected and the consequence of noncompliance. We don't make students go to time-out; they make themselves go by choosing to continue to misbehave. Having the choice gives students a feeling of control, which makes them more likely to choose appropriate behavior. The only time the language of choice is useless is when the misbehavior is so disruptive or potentially dangerous that the student must be removed from the room immediately.

The Who Squad Sooner or later, every teacher faces a student who is 100-percent recalcitrant. "You can't make me go to time-out," says the all-star quarterback to his five-foot teacher. At this point, the teacher can give a second choice: "Would you like to go by yourself, or would you like me to get someone who will help you go?" If the student continues to refuse to budge, it's time to call in the who squad.

Every school should designate pairs of staff members as the who squad, suggest Stanley Dubelle and Carol Hoffman in their book *Misbehavin'*.[1] Anyone strong and willing can serve on this squad—administrators, counselors, teachers, custodians. The squad can be rotated depending on people's schedules. Many secondary schools train teachers in crisis intervention techniques. The schools set up systems to cover these teachers' classes temporarily when a who squad situation occurs.

When called for by a teacher, the who squad walks into the classroom and asks, "Who?" The teacher indicates the student, and the who squad whisks him or her away. Once students know that they can't get away with outright defiance, few will bother trying it. If, however, the student will not move at the who squad's first request, or if the student threatens the safety of the teacher or the class, the who squad leader asks the teacher to move the class to another part of the building. With the audience gone and only the who squad left, even the most recalcitrant student will usually comply.

The who squad should be called immediately whenever a teacher feels physically threatened by a student. This is not a time for graceful exits or negotiation. Safety comes first.

Setting the Duration for Time-Out

The idea behind time-out is not to isolate students for great lengths of time. Rather, it gives them time and space, away from others, to cool down. Young students or first offenders can be given five minutes, while older students or repeat offenders might merit fifteen to thirty minutes. An alternative to setting the duration ourselves is to tell the student to return when she or he is ready to rejoin the group and behave appropriately.

If a student resumes misbehaving following a time-out, increase the length of the next time-out. Don't offer this student the option of setting the limit. If the student still continues to misbehave, try another location and use consequences in addition to time-out.

Having students devise a reentry plan while in time-out is a positive way to focus them on the future and keep them productively occupied. The purpose of a reentry plan is to lay the foundation for future classroom success by having students commit themselves, verbally or in writing, to more positive choices of behavior. The reentry plan can be as simple as a young child's orally completing the statement "What I will do differently in class is _____." Or, it can be as involved as a secondary student completing a Student Action Plan.[2]

When your back is against the wall, it's nice to know there's a "who squad" to call on.

The Resolution Stage: Set Consequences

In the physical world, every action has an automatic reaction. Turn over a glass of milk (action) and out spills the milk (reaction). Put your hand on a hot stove and you get burned. Since students are familiar with learning through natural action-reaction sequences, misbehaviors (actions) can be paired with unpleasant consequences (reactions) so that students can learn from experience.

The sequence of action and reaction in the classroom isn't quite as automatic as it is in physical science, however. Usually we have to arrange for the appropriate consequence to occur.

Guidelines for Effective Consequences

An effective consequence is "related, reasonable, and respectful," as noted by Jane Nelsen in *Positive Discipline*.[3] A fourth guideline, *reliably enforced*, adds to the effectiveness of the chosen consequence.

Related Consequences A related consequence is logically connected to the misbehavior. The more closely related the consequence and misbehavior, the more valuable the experience for the student. If Betsy continuously tips back her chair (misbehavior), she can be asked to stand for a set period (consequence). Betsy learns, "When I tip my chair back, I lose the privilege of sitting in it." A consequence of missing recess or staying after school would not be logically related to Betsy's misbehavior.

To maintain an appropriate relationship between the action and the consequence, we must establish consequences that take place at school, not at home. Some teachers are bothered by this because they like parents to get involved in the discipline process. But enforcing consequences for school misbehavior is not a parental responsibility. Imagine how we'd respond if parents called on us to enforce consequences for misbehaviors that occurred at home: "Miss Van de Berg, Sam failed to make his bed this morning. Would you please take away his playground privileges as a consequence?"

Reasonable Consequences A reasonable consequence is equal in proportion and intensity to the misbehavior. We use consequences to teach students to behave appropriately, not to make them suffer. For example, suppose Cassandra has scribbled her name on a lavatory door. A reasonable consequence would be to have her scrub that door. An unreasonable consequence would be to have her scrub every door in the washroom. Although the latter would be an unforgettable lesson, the increase in her hostility level would not be worth it. Our goal is to have a cooperative student, not a lifelong enemy.

Respectful Consequences A respectful consequence is stated and carried out in a way that preserves a student's self-esteem and doesn't discourage belonging through positive behavior. It contains no name-calling, blaming, shaming, or implied moral judgment. It is not accompanied by lectures or discussions about behavior. Rather, the consequence is stated in polite, unemotional, matter-of-fact terms.

Reliably Enforced Consequences Consequences lose their effectiveness when teachers don't follow through and enforce them. What we say *will* happen *must* happen. Otherwise students perceive that they are free to continue choosing irresponsible behavior with impunity. We need to be aware of a number of clever tactics students use to deflect us from reliably enforcing consequences:

Tactic 1: Buttering Up All students know how to give a compliment, offer a helping hand, and express appreciation when it's in their best interest. Every student also knows that teachers often find it difficult to enforce consequences when students seem so friendly and compliant.

Tactic 2: Promises, Promises Most young people know that adults can't resist good intentions, even when our experience tells us that promises often are all talk and no action.

Tactic 3: I'm Sorry Most students also know teachers can't resist apologies. Saying "I'm sorry" certainly may be appropriate, but an apology by itself does not take the place of a consequence.

Tactic 4: Invoking Guilt A reminder from students about difficult home situations or poor treatment by others can make us feel guilty, especially when their tone of voice and body language express sadness. Keep in mind that your goal is *not* to encourage students to feel like victims, but to help them choose productive behavior.

Tactic 5: Competition "When I was in Mr. Chen's class he didn't keep me away from the computer lab just because I didn't finish my report." Unfavorable comparisons, stated openly or merely implied, can shake our resolve to enforce consequences reliably.

Selecting the Consequence

Jerrold Gilbert has performed a valuable service by classifying consequences into four helpful categories: loss or delay of privileges, loss of freedom of interaction, restitution, and reteaching the appropriate behavior.[4] Practitioners of Cooperative Discipline have found the classifications to be effective in selecting consequences in the classroom.

Loss or Delay of Privileges
This consequence category includes the loss or delay of activities and the use of objects as well as loss of access to areas of the school.

Loss or delay of activity. When students misuse time through tardiness, dawdling, or disruption, we can deny or delay an activity they enjoy such as free time, recess, or a field trip. Students also could be required to come early or stay after school as a payback for the squandered time. The loss or delay can be proportionate to the amount of time misused, and increased each time the same or similar behavior occurs.

Keeping students from going to special classes such as physical education, music, art, or industrial arts is not a reasonable consequence. Special classes should not be considered subjects of lesser importance that can be withheld because of misbehavior elsewhere.

Loss or delay of using objects. Students who misuse books, laboratory apparatus, audiovisual equipment, sporting goods, or other objects can be deprived of their use for a limited time.

Loss or delay of access to school areas. When students misbehave in certain areas, such as the lunchroom or library, these can become off-limits to them for a reasonable amount of time.

Loss of Freedom of Interaction
This consequence might mean the loss of interactions with friends or required interactions with adults.

Denied interactions with other students. A student misbehaving for the sake of the audience can be isolated and denied interactions with peers for a short period of time. The time-out strategies already discussed are most effective for this purpose.

Required interactions with school personnel. When we are at an impasse with a student, we may want to require a meeting with the principal, guidance counselor, or dean. The purpose is to talk about what has happened and to come up with a plan so it doesn't happen again.

Select consequences that are:
Related
Reasonable
Respectful
Reliably enforced

Required interactions with parents. Some misbehaviors require an interaction with a parent or guardian. This was the case with Duane, a third grader who destroyed a classmate's art project. I took Duane with me to the phone, called his mother, and asked him please to tell her what he had done. I didn't ask Duane's mom to apply consequences at home for this in-school problem. The phone call was simply to inform her that the misbehavior had occurred.

Required interactions with police. Sometimes confrontive students break the law, perhaps through vandalism, stealing, dealing drugs, or bringing weapons to school. We should not shield these students from the legal consequences of their actions, for that only teaches them to "beat the system."

When we call in the police, we still have an obligation to help the young offenders choose appropriate behavior in the future. We'll want to use encouragement strategies to raise their self-esteem and to help them relate in positive ways to teachers and classmates. We'll also want to ask school support services—counselors, psychologists, and social workers—to work with the students and their families.

Restitution In her excellent book *Restitution*,[5] Diane Gossen defines restitution as an appropriate payback for irresponsible behavior. Restitution is used in Cooperative Discipline as a consequence that requires students to find ways to lessen the negative impact of their irresponsible choice. Restitution can be subdivided into three categories, depending upon whether the irresponsible behavior is related to objects, people, or time.

Return, repair, or replacement of objects. This category of restitution presents students with consequences that are both logical and tangible.

Objects "borrowed" without permission must be returned. If, for any reason, this isn't possible, then the objects in question must be replaced.

Students can make restitution for physical damage to school property by performing a service that undoes the damage to the greatest extent possible. For example, students who scratch desks can sand and refinish them. Those who stuff toilets can mop floors. We may have to spend extra time supervising this work, but it's worth taking the time to teach responsibility.

Sometimes students slash tires, crack windows, rip library books, or break audiovisual equipment. Should students have to pay for the damage? Yes, if the money really comes out of their own pocket. No, if their family foots the bill. When the latter happens, students learn that they can cause as much trouble as they like, and the adults in their life will fix it up in the end. If students have no money of their own to pay for damage, they can contribute time doing custodial or clerical services at school. The wages normally paid for such work can be used to pay for the damage. Again, the extra supervision needed will be worth it in the end.

Repayment of time. Repayment of time, often called "time-owed," is an appropriate consequence when students have wasted class time with a verbal temper tantrum. The teacher simply keeps track of the instructional time lost and negotiates with the student as to when this time will be paid back.

Compensation to classmates and teachers. Sometimes the irresponsible behavior students choose does psychological harm. Name-calling, put-downs, humiliating, and excluding classmates from activities are all damaging to the classmate's self-esteem. Restitution as a consequence requires that students who inflict such psychological harm devise ways to make amends to the person they have hurt. Some forms this compensation could take include helping in some way (such as carrying books or helping with an assignment), giving "put-ups" or verbal praise, sharing a treat, or including the person in a favorite activity.

Avoid requiring one student to apologize to another. Forced apologies tend to be insincere, and as a result the problem is prolonged. Focus instead on behavioral changes and plans for future positive interactions between the students involved.

School service. Students who repeatedly misbehave steal from the entire school community. They rob teachers and classmates of their right to teach and learn in a peaceful, positive atmosphere. Therefore it's logical to require these students to perform some type of school service that enhances the school environment as a payback for what they have stolen. In some secondary schools, the type and amount of school service is determined by a student judicial court whose function is to help misbehaving students learn to make more responsible choices. In other schools, a student council, faculty committee, or individual teacher might make this decision. The more we involve the misbehaving student in deciding the type and amount of school service, the more likely we are to win cooperation from this student in the future.

Reteach Appropriate Behavior

The ways to apply the consequence of reteaching appropriate behavior are to provide extended practice and to assign a written report.

Extended practice. No matter how many times you've asked Tamika not to slam her desk and run to the doorway when the bell rings, knocking into classmates on the way, she continues to do it "her way." The technique of extended practice allows her to practice the appropriate behavior—closing her desk quietly and walking slowly—until it is perfected. *When* the positive practice takes place isn't as important as reliably enforcing this consequence. Sooner or later, as the old adage says, practice makes perfect.

Restitution requires students to devise ways to make amends.

Written reports. In the old days, teachers often required misbehaving students to write "I will not _____" one hundred times. We know from experience this technique doesn't have much impact on today's students. A variation that works well, however, especially with secondary students, is to assign a written report that is logically connected to the misbehavior and emphasizes the value of making the more appropriate choice.

Suppose, for example, Kamala continually misuses the computer despite all your efforts to teach her how to use the machine correctly. Before you allowed her to return to the computer, you might ask Kamala to do a written report on the subject of floppy disks, including such topics as how they are manufactured, what problems result from misuse, and what it costs to replace disks. The knowledge this student gains in preparing the report will reinforce the appropriate behavior of using the computer with care.

Students' Response to Consequences

Many students with power and revenge behaviors respond to consequences by putting on a show of nonchalance to preserve their pride in front of peers and to keep us from seeing that we've reached them. They hope an "I don't care" attitude will persuade us to remove the consequences. Don't be fooled by this mask of indifference. Whether the student lets on or not, truly appropriate consequences will have a beneficial effect.

The Resolution Stage: Conduct a Teacher-Student Conference

The purpose of this conference is to confer with the student to resolve the conflict and create a plan for assuring more responsible behavior in the future. The steps to effective conferencing, including how to confer with students who are defiant and refuse to respond, are discussed in detail in Chapter 19.

Notes

1. Stanley Dubelle, Jr., and Carol Hoffman, *Misbehavin': Solving the Disciplinary Puzzle for Educators* (Lancaster, PA: Technomic Publishing, 1984), 49.
2. Presently many educators are reporting success with requiring reentry procedures before suspended students are allowed to return to the classroom. Typically, these require the student to meet with teachers, the counselor, and the administrator. The Student Action Plan provides an excellent vehicle for reentry conferences.
3. Jane Nelsen, *Positive Discipline* (New York: Ballantine, 1987), 67.
4. Jerrold Gilbert, "Logical Consequences: A New Classification," *Journal of Individual Psychology* 42 (no. 2):243. The original categories relate to consequences at home, and they have been adapted somewhat to apply more directly to school situations.
5. Diane Chelsom Gossen, *Restitution* (Chapel Hill, NC: New View Publications, 1993).

Dealing With Power and Revenge Behavior

Choose 1 Graceful Exit:

•Acknowledge students' power   •Remove the audience   •Table the matter
•Use a fogging technique: Agree, change subject, state both viewpoints, refuse responsibility, dodge irrelevant issues, closing statement, call student's bluff, teacher time-out

Success

No further action needed now

Options*

Consequences   Conference

Momentary Nonsuccess

Choose another graceful exit

Success

No further action needed now

Options*

Consequences

Conference

Momentary Nonsuccess or Escalation

Time-out   Referral

Options*

Consequences

Conference

Reentry conference

Encouragement

Assumptions
1. Intervention used correctly
2. Guidelines for avoiding and defusing confrontations (Chapter 8) followed
3. Emergency preparedness steps taken

---

* *Options can be used when teacher feels graceful exit not sufficient to influence student not to repeat misbehavior in future.*

CHAPTER 10

More About Revenge Behavior

Revenge behavior probably provokes the most difficult kind of teacher-student interaction. Since revenge behavior is not only disruptive but also destructive, our intense personal response may get in the way of effective action. We may even get to the point where we simply can't stand the student. As a result, we may be unable to discipline with the necessary impartiality.

Forming Relationships With Students We Dislike

We may not be able to like revengeful students, but we can learn to coexist peacefully with them. They have the right to be treated with dignity and respect. The following strategies will help us do that. They'll take some time and effort to carry out, but the results will be worth it. The changes start with us, the professionals—not with the students.

Change Our Perceptions Finding the good in revengeful students is like panning for gold—we may have to sift through pail after pail of muck to find the sparkle. One shortcut to gaining the gold is to begin perceiving weaknesses as strengths. The key to this is using positive language in place of negative words. For example, we may think of Sebastian as "stubborn" until we check a thesaurus and find such positive synonyms as *steadfast*, *resolute*, and *persistent*. If we start thinking of Sebastian's behavior in these terms, our perceptions can change for the better. Using positive language can help us interact more effectively with revengeful students:

We can change our perceptions of students we dislike.

> *Mr. Omoto asks Dorinda to stop tapping her pencil, and she substitutes her pen. When he puts a stop to this, she uses her ruler. Then her fingers. At this point, Mr. Omoto could get angry at Dorinda's deviousness. Or he could say, "Dorinda, your creativity is too much for me. I can't possibly think of everything. Would you help me out and not tap anything?" Once Dorinda's behavior is given a positive label, she can stop misbehaving without losing face.*

Change Our Reactions In a later chapter, we'll learn about the "Five A's" of encouragement: acceptance, attention, appreciation, affirmation, and affection. I can hear the howls now: "How can I possibly shower students I dislike with any of those A's?"

The task may seem bitter medicine at first. But if we can manage to swallow our dislike while we use encouragement strategies regularly for about a week or two, the relationship between us and the students is likely to change for the better. The students will perceive us differently, feel a greater sense of belonging, and probably respond more positively toward us. In turn, we'll feel more positive toward them.

Act Confident in Our Ability We need to appear confident. Revenge-seeking students typically take advantage of any perceived weakness. If we don't feel confident, we can at least act that way, pretending that we can handle confrontations with relative ease. If we do this consistently, we may even start to feel confident.

Demonstrate That We Care As Dubelle and Hoffman point out in *Misbehavin'*, our students don't need our love, but rather our care. We can't love them all, but we can show them all that we care what happens to them.[1] Caring is an action, not a feeling; it's something we do on behalf of the students. We can control our actions, even if our feelings are contrary. We can show our caring by taking steps to help revengeful students connect, contribute, and feel capable.

Caring is an action, not a feeling.

Teaching Students to Deal With Their Emotions

Revenge-seeking students can be greatly helped if they are taught how to vent their intense emotions safely. They will then have less need to lash out in hostility.

Verbalizing Feelings

During revenge interactions, we can ask students to tell us what they are feeling. If they're unwilling to answer directly, we can take a guess: "Looks to me like you're feeling upset and angry today." If our guess is wrong, students usually will correct us. If they admit we're right, we can express a willingness to hear more about it.

When we're caught in a situation in which an immediate discussion about feelings would be inappropriate, we can acknowledge the student's emotions and set a time to talk later. It's often helpful to ask students to write down or tape-record how they feel at the moment, and then use that information as a starting point for the subsequent discussion.

When we talk with students about emotions, our job is simply to listen and indicate that we hear what they are saying. We want to avoid telling students what they should or shouldn't feel or labeling their feelings as good or bad. To listen without giving advice or judgments is hard. It is helpful to remember the adage: "You have two ears and only one mouth. That means you should listen twice as much as you talk."

After students have expressed their feelings, we can ask, "What brings on these feelings?" If we're feeling brave, we can add, "Is there anything I do that makes you feel that way?" When students are willing to talk about which of our behaviors they find upsetting, we can learn a lot about our style of teaching and relating. If we think their comments are valid, we can make changes. If not, we needn't change a thing. We don't need to discuss the validity of the comments with the students. All we need do is thank them for being so candid and say that we'll think about what they've said.

Developing Anger Management Plans

It's normal for students to feel angry and frustrated at times. We can't expect these feelings to be discarded before students step into our classroom. Our challenge therefore is to develop anger management plans that help students find constructive ways to deal with these feelings so that they're not channeled into destructive outbursts and violent behavior.

Classroom Anger Management Plan Just as students need to know the accepted procedure for such tasks as completing assignments, standing in the lunch line, or signing out library books, they need to know the appropriate procedures for dealing with anger and frustration. We can conduct class discussions or class meetings to involve our students in devising these procedures, which then become known as our classroom anger management plan.

In elementary schools, many teachers set up a corner of the room where angry students can physically vent their feelings by drawing, pounding clay, throwing beanbags, or even tearing up old newspapers. In the same corner young students can verbally vent their feelings into a tape recorder or by "talking to teddy bear." Watching and talking to classroom pets often helps younger children calm down and get their anger and frustration under control. Parameters can be established in advance so that other students are not disturbed.

Secondary students may be able to manage their anger and frustration by moving to a study carrel or "peace table" in the classroom. Writing down their feelings often helps them regain control of themselves. Often, however, teenagers are better able to manage their anger outside the classroom. When the anger is relatively mild, a walk to the water fountain and a few deep breaths may ease their tension. When the anger is strong, a specific place needs to be designated where students can safely vent. Sometimes a counselor, phys. ed.

Teachers, too, need physical outlets for upsetting feelings.

teacher, or even a principal will maintain such a space. A punching bag in the gym, for example, can be a well-used emotional outlet.

Many classroom anger management plans with older students include an agreed-upon signal that students can use to indicate the need to get away from the class and regain personal control. Flashing a referee's time-out sign, showing a special pass, or tugging on an ear can suffice as long as the teacher and student have agreed on the signal in advance.

Personal Anger Management Plan For some young people, especially those with a history of severe behavior problems, more than the classroom anger plan is needed. These students need to be helped to understand their own aggressive and impulsive reactions when experiencing anger and frustration. They need to be led through a process that helps them answer these questions:

- What triggers my anger?
- What are my body responses to anger?
- How do I deal with my anger?
- What are the results?
- Is my approach effective?
- If not, what else could I do?[2]

When conferencing with revenge-seeking students, teachers can lead them through this process or refer them to a school counselor or social worker who can help them learn how to channel their anger and frustration in constructive ways.

Implementing Mediation Programs

Mediation puts the responsibility for solving interpersonal problems with the students.

Mediation programs that teach students how to handle interpersonal conflicts provide another channel for helping revenge-seeking students. Peer authority generally meets less resistance than adult authority, especially in secondary schools. It puts the power and responsibility for solving interpersonal problems where it belongs—with the students. The procedures used to devise nonviolent solutions to conflict teach aggressive and violence-prone students acceptable ways to handle negative feelings and impulsive actions.

Applying Intervention Techniques

When students attack us with hurtful deeds rather than words, we can use the same intervention techniques that we use during power confrontations. Revengeful students, however, are likely to be a bit more stubborn, and therefore dealing with them will probably take more time than with students who seek power.

When using time-out as an intervention for revenge behavior, send the student to a designated place outside of the classroom.

Separation from the teacher and the classroom gives the student a necessary cooling-off period. Make sure a who squad is available in case the student refuses to budge.

When using consequences, be sure to make them related, reasonable, respectful, and reliably enforced. Revengeful students always have their antennae up, just waiting for us to do something to justify their lashing out again.

Notes

1. Stanley Dubelle, Jr., and Carol Hoffman, *Misbehavin': Solving the Disciplinary Puzzle for Educators* (Lancaster, PA: Technomic Publishing, 1984), 53.
2. Adapted from *Handling Student Conflicts: A Positive Approach* (Miami: Grace Contrino Abrams Peace Education Foundation, 1993).

CHAPTER 11
Characteristics of Avoidance-of-Failure Behavior

We may fail to recognize avoidance-of-failure as a goal of misbehavior, since the student who is avoiding failure generally does not distract us or disrupt our classroom:

Alberto is slumped in his chair in the corner of the last row. He hasn't once looked at the Spanish words Ms. Alvarez has written on the board. When she asks why he isn't copying the words in a notebook like the other students, Alberto avoids eye contact. He shrugs his shoulders and sinks farther down in his seat.

Ms. Alvarez worries about Alberto. He never responds to her questions in class or to her kind remarks between classes. His cumulative folder indicates he has the ability to learn Spanish, but his poor classwork and incomplete homework present a contrary picture. Ms. Alvarez would like to help Alberto someday. But for now, with so many rowdy and disorderly students to worry about, she's relieved that at least he doesn't add to the disturbance.

Students like Alberto don't cause as much trouble as those who are seeking attention, power, or revenge. They tend to observe school rules and requirements. The problem is that they seldom interact with teachers and peers, choosing to remain isolated in the classroom, halls, and lunchroom. Another problem is that adults may view these students as "transparent." If we are not careful, we may look through these students as if they are nonexistent.

Sometimes a student needs to withdraw temporarily, to look within and regroup. Don't mistake temporary withdrawal for avoidance-of-failure behavior. Withdrawal becomes a problem when the student consistently engages in such behavior over a period of time, in ways that impede academic and social development.

The message of a student who fears failure is, "Leave me alone."

Active Avoidance-of-Failure

Avoidance-of-failure isn't usually active. The problem seldom lies in what the student is doing but rather in what the student is not doing.

One active avoidance-of-failure behavior is the frustration tantrum. On the surface this tantrum resembles a temper tantrum: Young students kick and cry, older students pound the desk and utter unprintable words. The goal of each type of tantrum is different, however. The temper tantrum is an *explosion* designed to get the teacher to back off and submit to the student's demands. In contrast, the frustration tantrum is an *implosion* designed to let off steam and direct the focus away from an apparent or potential failure. Students who have frustration tantrums have set out to perform certain tasks but have been unable to succeed to their own satisfaction. Finally, out of sheer frustration, they turn up the vocal volume or collapse into tears, hoping that the emotional outburst will allow them to avoid facing their failure.

Another active avoidance-of-failure behavior is clowning or goofing off. Underneath these antics is the hope that teachers and classmates will focus on the surface behaviors and not even notice the fear underneath.

Passive Avoidance-of-Failure

In most cases, students who seek to avoid failure exhibit this misbehavior passively.

Procrastination and Noncompletion

Some students—especially bright, capable youth—procrastinate to avoid failure. "I could have if I would have" is their motto. Most people have used this motto on a few occasions. Did you ever delay writing a paper until the night before it was due? Then, if you received a C, what did you tell yourself? Probably something like this: "I'm really a good student, and I could have gotten an A if I had worked harder." If instead you had worked for weeks on the paper and received a C, you might have thought, "Why not procrastinate and end up feeling like a winner, instead of working hard and feeling like a failure?"

Some students avoid failure by developing temporary incapacities.

Neglecting to complete projects and assignments is another variation of this passive avoidance-of-failure. Projects that are never finished cannot be judged or graded, so failure is impossible. I laughed when I learned about this kind of avoidance behavior because at the time I had a drawer full of half-sewn garments. I believed that smart people sewed to avoid the high cost of clothing. I had told myself, "I'm really okay at this. Someday I'll finish the clothes." If I had actually finished the sewing and nothing had fit, I'd have had to tell myself, "I guess I'm really a failure at sewing." By not completing the projects, I was able to continue feeling competent.

Temporary Incapacity

Some students avoid failure by developing temporary incapacities. For example, consider Morrie:

> *Morrie is skilled academically but feels klutzy in physical education classes. When it's time for phys. ed., he complains of a headache one time, stomach cramps the next—any ailment that might excuse him from a situation in which he expects to do poorly. Since he doesn't participate, no one can judge his performance. It's no surprise that Morrie's illness disappears as soon as phys. ed. is over.*

Assumed Disabilities

The current emphasis on learning disabilities and attention-deficit disorder inadvertently helps students successfully carry out avoidance-of-failure behavior. The whole notion of disabilities, especially when drugs are used as part of the corrective procedures, feeds into a student's notion of "I can't" and provides a seemingly legitimate excuse to withdraw and quit trying.

Even the most astute diagnostician has difficulty differentiating between real and assumed disabilities. Some students are so good at pretending, even on tests, that teachers often wonder if students *can't* or if they simply *won't*. Frequently, the students themselves don't really know. To make matters more confusing, some students who do have a minor disability have learned to make it major. By appearing more disabled than they are, these students can keep teachers at bay and thus avoid more failure.

Some students do need special help to learn. Unfortunately, the labels schools apply to them tend to reinforce these children's notions of their inadequacies. What they need is to be taught with methods and materials adapted to their needs and to hear the message, "You can do it!" When they receive consistent encouragement, their self-esteem will grow and they'll have less need to work at avoiding failure.

At times, students go to such lengths to procrastinate that we may not realize their goal is to avoid failure.

How to Identify Avoidance-of-Failure Behavior

We've learned three clues for distinguishing attention, power, revenge, and avoidance-of-failure goals: the reading on our emotional pressure gauge, our typical reaction, and the student's response to our correction.

Avoidance-of-Failure Clue 1: When faced with avoidance-of-failure behavior, our pressure gauge changes location, moving from deep inside our gut to our head. The readings on the gauge swing away from the mild-to-boiling scale. Instead of upsetting feelings like irritation, anger, and hurt, we'll feel *professional concern, frustration, perhaps despair.* We ask ourselves, "Why are our teaching strategies not working?" "Is there an undiagnosed learning disability?" Feeling that we simply can't get through to this student, we might even begin to doubt our own teaching ability.

Avoidance-of-Failure Clue 2: A typical reaction is to *give up* trying, feeling that we're up against a brick wall that we don't seem able to penetrate. We may seek a referral to the school support-service personnel as the only solution to the problem.

Avoidance-of-Failure Clue 3: When teachers give up trying and leave the student alone, the misbehavior doesn't stop temporarily (as with attention), nor does it intensify on the student's own terms (as with power or revenge). Rather, the young person's response is usually *to continue to avoid the task* at hand.

Origins of Avoidance-of-Failure Behavior

A number of all-too-prevalent social and educational factors contribute to students' choosing avoidance-of-failure behavior.

Rule of the Red Pencil

Students who behave to avoid failure look disabled, feel inadequate, and fear failure.

A long-accepted educational practice has been to mark students' mistakes in red pencil, with the number wrong clearly circled at the top of the page. Students know their mistakes are going to receive attention. Often everyone else in the class knows just how many mistakes they've made. No wonder some students simply decide not to do any work.

Unreasonable Expectations

When parents, teachers, or students have unreasonable expectations for success, avoidance-of-failure behavior soon follows. Realizing they can't reach the goal, students simply refuse to try. They'd rather be chastised for not making the effort than be branded "stupid" for trying and failing. They may see peers or siblings succeeding easily; when they compare their own stumbling efforts, they come up short. We may try to tell these students we'll be satisfied if they put forth their best effort, but they're not convinced. To refuse to try is less damaging to their ego than to try to achieve results that might not be satisfactory.

Perfectionism and Star Mentality

Students who strive to be perfect can't tolerate the slightest mistake. To them, an error isn't a normal part of the learning process but rather a tragedy to be avoided at all costs. How sad that so many bright, capable young people refuse to put forth any effort because they believe that only perfect performance is acceptable.

Society and schools usually recognize *results*, rarely the effort involved. The class valedictorian is honored for earning the highest grades, regardless of whether it took hard work to earn them. In contrast, who recognizes students like Tami, who went from a D-minus to a B-plus average by spending every afternoon with tutors? Or Whitney, who now comes to class on time and pays attention nearly the whole period?

Until they gain recognition, students will continue to choose avoidance-of-failure.

Emphasis on Competition

An emphasis on competition in the classroom is another reason some students adopt avoidance-of-failure behavior. If they have to be branded a winner or loser, they'd rather not play at all.

Some educators are champions of competition. They believe that competition motivates students to try harder and prepares them for real-life competition. But real-life competition differs from classroom competition, particularly in one major aspect: choice of arena. When we compete in the workplace, most of us are in our chosen field, doing work for which we have a preference and an aptitude—factors that give a competitive edge. For example, when I propose a book to a publisher, I know I'm competing against other authors, but I also know that I have the talent for writing such a book and hence a reasonable chance for success. I would never tell a clothing manufacturer, "I'd like to design dresses for you."

Students, however, are placed in a less fortunate position constantly. All day long, they're compared with other students in different subjects and skills, from math to English to social studies to science to physical education. They don't get to choose which subjects they'd like to compete in. They aren't allowed to say, "No thank you, Mr. Umbermeyer, I don't wish to compete in English today." So they speak with their behavior instead. They withdraw, isolate themselves, and refuse to try.

Students' Legitimate Needs

When we closely examine avoidance-of-failure behavior, we find that students who choose these behaviors have some immediate needs they do not know how to satisfy in appropriate ways. Like all of us, these students need to believe in themselves and to feel successful in their daily lives. They need to believe they are smart enough that, with good teaching from us and a reasonable effort from them, they will be able to succeed academically.

Avoidance-of-Failure Behavior's Silver Lining

Failure is an event, not a person.

For some students, ambition is the silver lining in avoidance-of-failure behavior. They want to succeed in school—if they can be assured of not making mistakes and of achieving some status. With the right strategies, we can nurture this ambition and help the students change their behavior.

For many students with avoidance-of-failure behaviors, however, there is no silver lining. These students are too discouraged. They have incredibly low self-esteem, and they lack the support of friends. Since they have no resources for going it alone, they need and deserve immediate help.

Principles of Prevention

Two principles of prevention are helpful for alleviating avoidance-of-failure behavior:

1. **Encourage an "I can" belief.** We must take every opportunity available to help these students change their self-perception from "I can't" to "I can."

2. **Foster friendships.** We can take an active role in ending failure-avoiding students' isolation by drawing them into congenial relationships with us and with other students.

In Chapters 13 and 14 we will look closely at ways we can put these principles into practice.

CHAPTER 12
When the Goal Is Avoidance-of-Failure: Interventions

W e can rarely pinpoint the exact moment of avoidance-of-failure behavior since such behavior usually doesn't disrupt our lessons, distract our attention, or destroy property. Students who fear failure simply don't do their schoolwork, quietly hoping we won't notice. While we eventually need to help them connect and contribute to make a real difference in their school performance, our first step is to help these students feel capable and be successful.

Intervention techniques that help students feel capable can be grouped into ten strategies.

> *It's better to try and fail than fail to try.*

The First Five Strategies

We'll begin with Strategies 1-5, which are specifically tailored to students who fear failure. The other five intervention strategies are also encouragement strategies. They are helpful for all children but particularly useful with students fearful of failure. Strategies 6-10 are summarized in this chapter and fully explained in Chapter 13.

Strategy 1: Modify Instructional Methods
Four techniques are recommended for modifying instructional methods: using concrete learning materials, using computer-assisted instruction, teaching one step at a time, and changing the modality by teaching to the seven types of intelligence.

Use Concrete Learning Materials Many students learn best when they use materials that they can see, feel, and manipulate. Over sixty years ago, Maria Montessori proved that youngsters considered failures by their parents and teachers could, with the right materials, succeed academically as well as their so-called brighter peers. To produce these spectacular results, Montessori designed and used concrete learning materials that met these criteria:

- Attractive—Students love working with materials that are interesting and colorful.
- Self-explanatory—Students are motivated to work when they can determine independently how the materials are used.
- Self-correcting—Students discover that making mistakes is natural and okay when no one else has to know how many errors they make while learning a new skill.

- Reusable—Students can practice tasks over and over again until they've achieved mastery. Then the same materials can be used again to give children the joy of succeeding repeatedly.

Learning materials that meet Montessori's four criteria are readily available for today's classroom.

Use Computer-Based Instruction Modern technology has provided an additional learning tool that adds a new dimension to teaching methods—the computer. Many students who wouldn't dream of picking up a pencil in class can sit for hours in front of a monitor, working on basic skills. Although not concrete, educational software does have the four characteristics of the Montessori learning materials.

Computers can't take our place, of course. And while all students can benefit from computer-assisted instruction, those who underachieve for fear of failure are particularly helped by it. The self-explanatory, self-correcting, and reusable features enable such students to take risks that they'd never chance with traditional instructional materials.

Teach One Step at a Time Students who are afraid of failure are easily overwhelmed. They can be frightened into passivity by a complex learning task that's appropriate for their classmates. We can entice these students to tackle the task if we break it up into small, progressive steps so that the chance of making errors is reduced. We can further help them by giving feedback after they complete each step. Each small success will spur them on, and each small mistake will be easier to correct than multiple mistakes involving the whole task.

Teach to the Seven Intelligences Picture yourself being forced to write with your nondominant hand for an extended period of time. Wouldn't it be a painful experience? Some of our students are experiencing "painful learning" when being taught *only* in our traditional educational delivery system, which consists of teaching mainly to the verbal/linguistic and logical/mathematical intelligences.

Howard Gardner has identified seven modes of intelligence and has recommended that we teach to all seven to help students succeed.[1] Finding the dominant mode of intelligence and switching to strategies that emphasize it helps a student with avoidance-of-failure behavior overcome discouragement. Some examples of teaching strategies and activities to accommodate each of the seven intelligences are:

- verbal/linguistic: journals, discussions, debates, television, computers, guest speakers, dramatic readings, jokes
- logical/mathematical: graphic organizers, outlines, analogies, problem-solving, mnemonics, research, labs, formulas

- visual/spatial: posters, charts, graphics, painting, drawing, demonstrations, computers, videos, television
- body/kinesthetic: role playing, creative movement and dance, field trips, physical exercise, games, projects
- musical/rhythmic: singing, raps, poems, cheers, limericks, choral reading, instruments
- intrapersonal: reflection, journals, independent assignments, thinking strategies, goal setting
- interpersonal: cooperative learning, group projects, interviews, cooperative games, joint storytelling, class meetings

Periodically integrating activities using the seven intelligences invites more students to work in their learning comfort zone. It exposes them to activities that might pique their interest and uncovers aptitudes in areas previously unexplored.

Strategy 2: Provide Tutoring

Many students who exhibit avoidance-of-failure behavior are caught in a failure chain. They have missed learning some basic academic skills, and this gap in skills makes schoolwork difficult and frustrating. Moreover, these students have lost confidence in trying to close the gap because they see classmates completing assignments with ease. As their confidence slips, so does their motivation, which leads to continued poor performance and more erosion of confidence.

Peer tutoring can help students connect, contribute, and feel capable.

At this point, the students can do little on their own to break the failure chain. Their best hope is tutoring in basic skills, which breaks the chain by erasing the gap, restoring confidence, and encouraging success. Five forms of tutoring are most beneficial for students who fear failure:

- extra help from teachers
- remediation programs
- adult volunteers
- peer tutoring
- commercial learning centers

Strategy 3: Encourage Positive Self-Talk

Students with avoidance-of-failure behavior often develop a pattern of negative self-talk. When faced with tasks, they may repeatedly think, "It's too hard" or "I'll never get this right." Such damaging put-downs can become self-fulfilling prophecies that stifle students' initiative and motivation. We can help students turn negative internal messages into positive self-talk by using several techniques.

> *"If you think you can or you think you can't, you're right."*
> *—Henry Ford*

Post Positive Classroom Signs "You can if you think you can!" was the message on the sign posted by Mrs. Jones, my ninth-grade algebra teacher way back when. I read that sign every day, and its positive words gradually began to counter my subconscious belief that I'd never do well in algebra. Little by little, the impact of my own negative self-talk was reduced, and my willingness to persevere with mathematics increased.

Plastering our classroom walls with positive self-talk signs takes little effort. Students can be asked to write—and perhaps illustrate—a number of such signs that can be rotated on a regular basis. Here are some possible messages for the signs:

- I can do it!
- With a little effort, I'll succeed.
- I'm smart enough to do good work.
- I can when I tell myself I can.
- I can change how I think and feel.

Require Two "Put-Ups" for Every Put-Down Initiate the rule that for every negative statement students say aloud about themselves, they must counter with two "put-ups," or positive statements. Such a practice not only helps students focus on the way they talk about themselves but also helps transform a negative self-image into a positive one. At first, students may feel a little foolish verbalizing good things about themselves. But with time and practice, put-ups usually become just as automatic as put-downs. And when this happens, the fear of failure diminishes.

Encourage Positive Self-Talk Before Tasks The "tape recorder" in students' heads begins playing as soon as an assignment is given. To ensure that the tape played is positive, we can ask students with avoidance-of-failure behavior to say aloud two positive things about the task at hand before they set out to tackle it: "I can do these problems with fractions" and "I'm smart enough to find all the answers."

If students get bogged down during the assignment, we can suggest that they repeat their positive statements under their breath. Students who learn consciously to "replay" the positive tape when they feel threatened by a task will usually achieve success. That success will make it easier to "eject" the negative tape and to insert the positive tape whenever they're dealing with an assignment.

Everyone can benefit from positive self-talk.

Strategy 4: Reframe the "I Can't" Refrain

"I can't" is a favorite refrain of students who fear failure. When presented with a task that seems the least bit difficult, they quickly give up and give in to this erroneous belief. Psychologists use the term *reframing* to mean changing perspective, taking a different point of view. We help students reframe their "I can'ts" in a couple of ways.

State Your Belief in Students' Abilities

Disagree with students' negative statement. Make responses such as:

- "Of course you can. How can I help you?"
- "Please repeat after me: 'I can't right now but I'm willing to learn how.'"
- "You have the ability. Now add some effort and your 'I can't' will become 'I can.'"

Stage an "I Can't" Funeral

The book *Chicken Soup for the Soul*[2] contains a marvelous description of a funeral conducted by a fourth-grade teacher:

The students are asked to fill a notebook page with "I can'ts," a list of all the tasks they believe they cannot do. The lists go into a box that is then literally buried in the dirt in the schoolyard, with a headstone and an epitaph that reads "I can't. RIP." In her eulogy, the teacher talks about the surviving siblings, "I will" and "I'm going to right away."

I envision the crypt for "I can't" like those in New Orleans. Because that city is below sea level, family crypts are built above the ground and can be opened to admit the remains of family members as they pass on. As new "I can'ts" creep into the classroom, they can be quickly buried and placed in the crypt with their "ancestors."

While secondary students might balk at the idea of an actual burial, they could write a play, produce a puppet show, or create a documentary or an ad campaign that illustrates these ideas. They can also take it one step further and present the work to elementary students.

Strategy 5: Teach Procedures for Becoming "Unstuck"

Everyone gets stuck at times, not knowing how to accomplish the task at hand. Teaching students procedures for becoming "unstuck" empowers them to continue working rather than quitting.

Brainstorm Ask-for-Help Gambits A *gambit* is an opening move, a beginning, a strategy. Some students stay stuck because they don't know how to begin to ask for help, especially in ways that don't attract unwanted attention from peers. During a class discussion or meeting, brainstorm with your students gambits they can use when help is needed. Do they simply want to raise their hands? use some other signal? sign their name on a clipboard kept on your desk?

Use Sequence Charts Depending upon our subject area, we can identify and chart a sequence of steps students can follow when they don't understand an assignment. The steps might include such things as rereading the directions, underlining key words, or doing the first two problems. As with the ask-for-help gambits, the more the students are involved in creating these sequence charts, the less afraid they'll feel when they do get stuck.

Five Additional Intervention Strategies: An Overview

Five intervention strategies that are also encouragement strategies useful with all students are especially helpful in working with those who fear failure.

> *"The greatest mistake a person can make is to be afraid of making one."*
> —Albert Hubberd

Make Mistakes Okay The fear of making mistakes keeps students stuck in the avoidance-of-failure rut. They interpret every mistake, no matter how small, as proof that they can't do anything right—ever. We can help them learn to accept mistakes as part of the learning process.

Build Confidence *Building confidence* means helping students who fear failure realize that success is possible. They need to believe they not only can perform tasks capably but also are successful just being themselves, regardless of their skill level.

Focus on Past Successes Every student has experienced some success. We may have to dig deep to find examples for students who avoid failure. But by repeatedly reminding these students of past successes, no matter how small, we can build a basis for effort that may lead to major achievements.

Make Learning Tangible If they can't see or touch something, many students think it doesn't exist. Unfortunately, "learning" is something that's hard to see or touch. For students who need sensory feedback to realize that learning has occurred, we have to make learning as tangible possible.

Recognize Achievement If students were to receive as much recognition for achievement as they do for failure, avoidance-of-failure behavior could be eliminated. Achievement or improvement in *any* area needs to be acknowledged. When students fearful of failure receive recognition from others, especially from teachers and classmates, they begin to feel capable and to believe that they can successfully connect and contribute.

Notes

1. Howard Gardner, *Frames of Mind: The Theory of Multiple Intelligences* (New York: Harper and Row, 1983).
2. Jack Canfield and Mark Victor Hansen, *Chicken Soup for the Soul* (Deerfield Beach, FL: Health Communications, 1993), 156-60.

*I*f our discipline program were to include only intervention strategies for the moment of misbehavior, we could be pretty sure that students would misbehave again—today, tomorrow, or the next day. The only way to end the misbehavior permanently is to raise students' self-esteem. The building blocks of self-esteem are the same Three Cs that help students feel they belong. When students believe they're *capable* and know they can *connect* and *contribute* successfully, they no longer need to engage in misbehavior to try to fulfill their need to belong.

Most encouragement strategies are neither difficult nor time-consuming.

We can teach students to satisfy the Three Cs through using encouragement strategies. Our positive response to appropriate behavior can do more to convince students to continue such behavior than will all the interventions in the world. Fortunately, most encouragement strategies are neither difficult nor time-consuming. We simply need to be aware of them and committed to using them daily.

As we implement encouragement strategies, we need to recognize that an important variable affects our ability to give encouragement—our emotional response toward a particular misbehavior. For example, giving lots of encouragement to students who fear failure is usually not difficult. These students don't disrupt our classroom, so our response to them is sympathetic. We naturally want to help them. On the other hand, giving even a normal level of encouragement to power-seeking students may seem challenging indeed. This is because our emotional response to these students is negative. If we keep in mind that our emotional response varies according to the behavior that's occurring at the moment, we will feel less discouraged as we try to encourage all our students.

While encouragement is important for all, some areas in which it can play an especially powerful role are worth noting.

Drop-out prevention. One of the most important factors in drop-out prevention is the amount of academic success a student experiences in middle school. The more we incorporate into our classroom's daily life these strategies to help students feel capable, the more successful students become.

Inclusion of special-needs students. Imagine you are a special-needs student who has just entered a mainstream classroom for the first time. Look around. You'll observe many classmates doing tasks that you haven't yet begun to learn. How discouraging that must feel!

Yet, to succeed in this placement, you need to feel just as capable as everyone else. While the strategies in this chapter will help *all* students feel capable, they are especially important in the mainstreamed classroom.

Violence prevention. Young people who find no success in the academic arena are prone to look elsewhere for the satisfaction that comes from succeeding. Unfortunately, all too many students find that they are extremely capable at fighting, stealing, vandalizing, and other forms of antisocial and criminal behavior. To reduce and prevent violence, therefore, we need to use as many of the strategies in this chapter as we can, as often as we can—especially with violence-prone students who seek revenge.

Motivator of Success: The "I-Can" Level

One of the most accurate predictors of success in school is a student's "I-can" level. The I-can level is a much more helpful motivator than the IQ level. With appropriate teaching, students who believe in their ability to master required learning tasks will usually succeed. Their success is not only academic but also emotional. They feel good about themselves because they've fulfilled one of the Three Cs—feeling capable.

Students with disabilities and special needs tend to have a low I-can level. As this level rises, so does the probability that these young people will reach their full potential. We can work toward raising *all* students' I-can levels by using the encouragement techniques described in this chapter. The techniques are grouped according to five major strategies.

Strategy 1: Make Mistakes Okay

The fear of making mistakes undermines a student's I-can level. When we remove this fear, we remove a great barrier to feeling capable. Several effective techniques can help us do this.

Talk About Mistakes Young people are often selective in their observations. They notice their own mistakes but not those of others. As a result, they become convinced that everyone else is better, smarter, and more capable than they. Our job is to revise this viewpoint by helping students understand that *everyone* makes mistakes.

When students begin to talk about mistakes, they soon discover that mistakes are a natural—and integral—part of the learning process. The game of "Classroom Password" provides an easy format for initiating such discussion. When the bell rings to signal lunch or to change classes, we can stand at the door and announce that the

As students watch others' mistakes, they discover strategies for dealing with their own.

password for leaving is to state one recent mistake. Any mistake will do, whether it occurred at home, on the bus, or in class.

At first, students probably won't appreciate this game. Since failure is so rarely talked about in the open, some students will be fearful of revealing their mistakes in front of others. To understand that their fear is groundless, students need to hear us admitting that we make mistakes too. By sharing our own mistakes with students, we can help them recognize that blunders are a normal part of everyone's life.

Once both we and our students become used to talking about mistakes, we can narrow the focus of the password: "Name one mistake you made in social studies and what you learned from that mistake. I'll start: I should have remembered that reference book I promised to bring to class."

Eventually, we can expand the password game by adding this question: "What can you do so you don't make the same mistake again?" Answering this helps students understand that the most important thing is not avoiding mistakes but being able to figure out what to do next.

Rewarding mistakes is one way to make the point that effort is valuable even when we fail.

Equate Mistakes With Effort We need to acknowledge that more mistakes are made by active people than by passive people and that active participation is desirable. Then we can actually reward mistakes with enthusiastic remarks, thus motivating students to continue working. Comments like these are appropriate when students who are really trying make mistakes:

- "You've made a mistake. So what? Now you know what to focus on. Let's see what can be learned from it."
- "This mistake is no big deal. After all, if you never made a mistake in English, I wouldn't have a job!"

Minimize Mistakes' Effects Correcting mistakes in students' schoolwork is part of our job. Yet to help students feel capable, we need to minimize the effect of making mistakes. To do this, we need to stop highlighting *every* error. Red-lined papers can be overwhelming to students, especially those who already have low self-esteem and feel incapable.

This doesn't mean that we can't give constructive criticism and ask students to correct mistakes. It just means that we begin the task of correction by breaking it down into easy steps that students are capable of completing. We can do this by having students focus on correcting only one or two errors or types of errors at a time.

Strategy 2: Build Confidence

Students must feel confident that success is possible. To help them build such confidence, we can use a number of techniques that emphasize positive feedback.

Focus on Improvement

If we wait until a student completes a task error-free before we say anything positive, we're likely to wait forever. If instead we devote more interest to the *process* of learning rather than the *product*, we'll notice and praise each small step forward.

When we note a student's improvement, we focus only on what the student can do tomorrow. We don't compare the student's work with anyone else's or with grade-level charts.

Notice Contributions

Students who fear failure may resist putting anything down on paper, because any errors will be permanently recorded for all to see. Their fear may not extend beyond the edge of the paper, however. Such students often are willing to participate actively in class discussions and group tasks. We can point out the usefulness of these contributions to the students, their classmates, and their families. Since being able to contribute is one of the Three Cs of belonging, we need to notice and encourage this behavior as much as possible.

Build on Strengths

Every student has some strength, no matter how well hidden. We noted earlier the importance of seeking the good in each student if we are to build healthy relationships. Likewise, we can seek out strengths on which to build academic skills. When we notice the gold shining through, we can tell the students directly or write it down on their papers. They need to hear about their strengths frequently and in detail.

While growing up, many of us were told that we'd get a "swelled head" if we bragged or said complimentary things about ourselves. What nonsense! If we can't talk about what we can do well, how can we possibly feel capable? The ability to recognize and talk about our strengths is a powerful motivator and self-esteem builder. We can help students focus on their strengths by playing a variation of Classroom Password, asking each student to mention a personal strength, positive characteristic, or talent before exiting the classroom at the end of the period or the day.

Show Faith in Students

Our faith in our students is reflected in our expectations. Low expectations demonstrate low confidence. Higher expectations indicate more confidence, as long as the expectations are realistic and the lessons appropriate. To demonstrate sincere faith in our students' capabilities, we can tailor activities to their abilities. Moreover, positive comments such as "You can handle it," "You

Today's contributions boost tomorrow's feelings of capability.

are the kind of students who can do this," and "I know you can do it" indicate our faith in our students.

Acknowledge a Task's Difficulty Many students, especially those trying to avoid failure, perceive any new learning task as difficult. We need to acknowledge their point of view. One way to do this is to avoid making light of a task by labeling it "easy." If students do fail at such an "easy" task, they naturally assume that they must be stupid. Instead, we need to support students' feelings while affirming their capabilities: "I know this is difficult. Keep at it a while longer. I bet you'll get the hang of it." When students do succeed at a task that we've labeled "difficult," their self-esteem gets a healthy boost.

Set Time Limits on Tasks When students know that work they perceive as difficult is not going to last forever, the task can seem easier to bear. If students *want* to continue working after the time is up, we can of course encourage them to do so. Our goal is to create a reasonable minimum time frame and thereby ease the stress that comes from facing difficult tasks.

Strategy 3: Focus on Past Successes

When I was growing up, my parents and teachers frequently pointed out what I was doing wrong, with the hope of motivating me to do better in the future. Today, many educational psychologists tell us that just the opposite is true. The way to motivate young people to succeed is to point out everything they do right. Success builds success, we are told, and we therefore should focus on students' past accomplishments to ensure that their good work continues.

Analyze Past Success We need to do more than just point out successes, says Bernard Weiner, developer of the attribute theory of success.[1] Weiner states that most of us attribute our successes to five factors: our belief in our ability, our effort, help from others, a task's difficulty, and luck. Students control only two of these factors—*their belief in their ability* and the *amount of effort they put out*. They cannot dictate how much help they will receive from others, how difficult the task will be, or whether luck will be on their side.

We can help students understand that the two factors they do control are the major components of success. We can ask them, "Do you know why you succeeded at that task?" If they reply that it was because they have "smarts" or tried so hard, we can reinforce their perceptions by agreeing with them. If their response is that it was because they got help, we can counter, "Yes, that's true, you did get help. But you put out the effort and proved you have the ability." If they say that the task was easy, we can respond, "Your ability and effort made it seem easy." If they claim it was just luck, we can say, "You make your own luck by using your ability and making the effort."

Focus on students' past accomplishments to ensure that their good work continues.

We can also challenge students to repeat the task again so they can prove to themselves that they created their own success. By continually analyzing past successes in this way, we not only help students believe in their own capabilities but also encourage them to keep making the effort to learn.

Repeat Past Success While moving forward to new learning tasks is important, standing still for a moment, savoring and repeating today's successes, is equally important. A familiar classroom phenomenon lends credibility to this observation—the enthusiasm that students display for doing old worksheets over and over again. Whether the task is worksheets or other types of assignments, when students have an opportunity to repeat yesterday's work, they use skills they have mastered, therefore making fewer mistakes and experiencing more success.

Strategy 4: Make Learning Tangible

One reason why some students don't believe in their capabilities is because they can't see their progress. Grades and test scores, the usual benchmarks for measuring progress, don't always give the necessary information. For example, a student who receives Cs for two consecutive marking periods might assume that no progress has been made. Young elementary students often receive only "satisfactory" or "unsatisfactory" marks, which reveal nothing about their progress. We need to switch from "Whadja get?" to "Whadja learn?"

"I-Can" Cans Young students can make "I-Can" cans by decorating large, empty coffee cans with construction paper or adhesive paper. In their cans, they deposit strips of paper on which they've written skills they've mastered, such as reading or spelling words and arithmetic facts. As their cans fill up, students can point with pride to all the new things they've learned. The I-Can can is also useful during parent conferences because it contains concrete evidence that a child is making progress.

Accomplishment Albums and Portfolios Older students can create an accomplishment album or portfolio[2] using a three-ring binder, paper, theme dividers, and decorations such as stickers and glitter. They can label the sections with headings such as "Math Problems I Can Solve," "Books I Have Read," or "French Verbs I Can Conjugate." Students can chart their progress by writing down new skills as they are mastered. The album concept also works well for just one subject area, with the headings reflecting appropriate categories for the subject. For example, an eighth-grade student's English album might include "New Vocabulary I've Mastered," "Grammar and Punctuation Rules I've Learned," "Literature I've Read," and "Writing

Young students love the recognition represented by stars and stickers.

Skills I've Demonstrated." A large manila envelope can be attached to the binder to hold examples of written work and art projects.

Students should never compare their accomplishment albums. The emphasis should be solely on individual growth, helping students see what they learned today that they didn't know yesterday. Accomplishment albums also are great aids during parent conferences since they are tangible records of student progress.

Checklists of Skills Many schools have established master lists of skills to be taught in each subject at each grade level. Teachers generally use these lists when preparing lessons and when writing reports on student progress for parents. Such checklists also are ideal for helping students feel capable. With each new skill they can check off, their I-can level rises.

Flowchart of Concepts A flowchart accompanies just about every commercially published academic program. The chart lists concepts and skills introduced in the program and describes where and when they appear. Most teachers use the flowchart primarily to plan lessons, but it can also be used in helping students plot progress. A chart may need to be simplified for use by young students, but even they can benefit from knowing where they are going, when they will get there, and which milestones they will pass along the way.

Talks About Yesterday, Today, and Tomorrow Useful in conjunction with any of the techniques suggested for Strategy 4 are frequent talks about yesterday, today, and tomorrow. For example, we can say to a student, "Remember when you weren't able to spell many words? Now look at how many words you have inside your I-Can can!" When we discuss the progress a student has made in such concrete terms, we increase confidence and self-esteem immeasurably. Moreover, failure doesn't seem so scary—or so inevitable—when we talk frequently about progress.

Talks about tomorrow based on past successes help students anticipate future success: "Look how many items on the checklist you've mastered this month. How many more do you think you'll be able to master next month?" Such anticipation is an excellent motivator for convincing students to stick to difficult tasks.

Strategy 5: Recognize Achievement

For students to continue to want to make progress, they must receive recognition from others for the progress they've already made. Here are some effective techniques for acknowledging achievements.

Applause is called for whenever students behave positively in a situation that previously caused them difficulty.

Applause Applause says, "Hooray for you! You did it!" When we give applause, we don't have to clap our hands, but our enthusiasm ought to be no less evident. We can applaud achievement in school and out, in both academic and nonacademic areas. Applause needs to be specific and nonjudgmental, without comparisons, and with no mention of past or future expectations.

One of the best ways to give applause is simply to notice the situation and reflect it back to the student:

- "Wow, Monica, look at how clearly you've outlined the causes leading up to the Civil War."
- "Congratulations, Paulo! I see your sketch was selected for the all-school exhibit."

Applause is called for whenever students exhibit positive behavior in a situation that previously caused them difficulty. For example, we notice that Monroe, who has been withdrawn in phys. ed., is finally taking an active part in a game. We can reinforce the good example he is setting for himself by saying, "Way to go, Monroe! I saw you cheering your teammates on while you waited for your turn."

Clapping and Standing Ovations We can encourage students to recognize classmates' achievements by clapping and giving standing ovations. The recipient feels noticed, appreciated, and special. Most students love taking center stage, even for just a moment. It costs nothing, takes little time, provides a change of pace, and releases pent-up energy for the entire class.

Stars and Stickers Young students love the recognition represented by stars and stickers. A happy face on a worksheet or a big golden star stuck on a shirt collar says, "I've noticed your achievement, and I'm proud of you." Do use stars and stickers sparingly so that students don't perceive them as the major reward for a job well done.

Awards and Assemblies All kinds of certificates and awards can be given out in homeroom, at lunch, or during assemblies. The more achievements we find to notice, the more positive the classroom atmosphere and the school environment become. Remember, however, to recognize increased effort and improved performance, not just "the best." One clever teacher takes unclaimed sneakers from the lost and found, paints them gold, and presents them to deserving students as "The Golden Sneaker Award for Runaway Effort."

Exhibits By means of bulletin boards, display cases, and presentations in other classrooms, we can advertise students' achievements. We can also invite parents to view special exhibits of student work, and we can submit announcements of student achievements to the local newspaper.

Positive Time-Out Everyone knows that students sent to time-out in the principal's office are in trouble. This negative image of the school administrator can be changed if we start sending students to the office for positive time-out, or to receive recognition for achievement from the principal. We can also send students to counselors, librarians, learning specialists, or volunteers for recognition. Positive time-out is a particularly powerful technique to use with students who are afraid to fail. When these students receive recognition from staff members, their low opinion of themselves starts changing for the better.

Classroom teachers can provide another kind of positive time-out. Taking a moment at the end of class to talk alone with a student who deserves recognition is a powerful motivator. We could also take a few minutes during lunch, free periods, or after school to deliver such praise. We don't have to do anything fancy during positive time-out, and it needn't take long. It's our presence and our undivided attention that mean so much to a student. Even older students appreciate a teacher's attention, although many wouldn't admit it for fear of being labeled "teacher's pet."

Self-Approval Teaching students to recognize their own achievements is vital. Otherwise, students may become approval-dependent, waiting for others to notice what they've done instead of looking inside for self-approval. One way we can promote self-approval is by

A positive learner self-concept depends on feeling capable.

asking each student to state a personal accomplishment that's worthy of recognition. In time, students learn to enjoy the good feelings that spring from talking about their accomplishments.

Notes

1. Bernard Weiner, "Principles for a Theory of Student Motivation and Their Application Within an Attributional Framework," in *Research on Motivation in Education: Student Motivation*, eds. R. E. Ames and C. Ames, vol. 1 (New York: Academic Press, 1984).
2. Linda Albert and Michael Popkin, *Quality Parenting* (New York: Random House, 1987), 105-6.

CHAPTER 14
Helping Students Connect

W e can help students feel connected with us by forming A+ relationships with them. An A+ relationship is one that involves plenty of *acceptance, attention, appreciation, affirmation,* and *affection.* When we model these five A's, we teach students how to initiate and maintain positive relationships with their peers. We also encourage them to become receptive to our efforts to discipline, to instruct, or to help in other ways. When we withhold the A's, students are likely to become uncooperative, resistant, and even hostile.

Older children and adolescents *will* feel the void created by the lack of A's in their lives. Earlier we noted that the need for connecting—for attaining the A's—is so important that many youth choose the "family" of the gang to fulfill this need.

The Five A's

This chapter discusses how we can administer doses of the "Five A's" in various ways that help students connect.

Acceptance

"The most critical behavior a child can experience is total acceptance as a person . . . the most growth-producing gift that can be given," writes Barbara Clark in *Growing Up Gifted.*[1] Even though we know that growth is an essential function of learning, we can't base our acceptance of students on the growth that they *might* or *should* or *must* make. We need to accept them wholeheartedly as they are right now—complete with quirks, flaws, and faults. Acceptance of each student must be sincere and unconditional; there is no substitute for authenticity in our relationships.

Acceptance is like an umbrella over the other four A's. It is the essential attitude that allows us freely to give attention, appreciation, affirmation, and affection.

We need to accept our students as they are—complete with quirks, flaws, and faults.

Accepting Students' Cultural Differences
In today's multicultural classrooms, we encounter a great variety of dress, speech, and mannerisms. Even so simple a matter as whether a student makes eye contact with us can be culturally determined. If we want students from different backgrounds to apply themselves academically and to choose responsible behavior, we have to accept these differences. By

not insisting that our students "be like us," we model accepting differences. Since students often model their behavior on ours, we lay the foundation for a classroom environment in which everyone can belong.

Accepting Students With Disabilities With more and more school districts moving toward the inclusion of students with disabilities into the regular classroom, we have to make these young people feel welcome despite their disabilities often meaning more work for us. The more we use the A's of attention, appreciation, affirmation, and affection to demonstrate acceptance of students with disabilities, the more willing our other students will be to befriend and to help students with differing abilities satisfy their need to belong.

Accepting Students' Personal Style Personal idiosyncrasies in dress or habits require a tolerant attitude. If individual quirks get in the way of classroom functioning, however, we may have to work out some kind of compromise with the students. We need to remember, though, that values do change from generation to generation, and what seems unacceptable to us may be the only way that students can fit in with their peers.

Accepting the Doer, Not the Deed Students need to believe they are still worthy human beings even when their behavior is inappropriate. This helps them retain enough self-esteem so they're able to choose more appropriate behavior in the future. Chapter 8 includes advice about how we can voice disapproval of a deed without rejecting the doer.

Attention

We give attention by making ourselves available to students, by sharing our time and our energy in meaningful ways. We can prevent a lot of classroom disruption by providing large doses of positive attention *before* misbehavior occurs. The time we take away from teaching to give attention is balanced by the time we save when we don't have to cope with misbehavior.

How can one teacher give personal attention to a class of twenty to thirty-five students and still cover the curriculum? Fortunately, many of the ways in which we can give quality attention require only a few moments. Yet the beneficial effects can be felt for hours or even days.

Greet Students The quickest and easiest way to make sure each student has a small bit of quality attention from us is to use the few moments before or after class to say a word or two to each individual. Yes, this means we must be organized enough not to need those few moments for last-minute preparation or cleanup. The extra effort is worth it. We're sure to get results, as Mrs. Murti discovered when she gave some quality attention to one of her kindergartners:

Damon was the class bully. Nothing Mrs. Murti did or said seemed to reach him. I suggested that she try giving him special attention by greeting him each morning with a compliment. Mrs. Murti seemed doubtful that she could find anything nice to say to Damon, so I suggested that she comment on his shirt—the color, the design, the buttons, whatever caught her eye. A few days later, she sent me a one-word message: "HELP!" I asked her what was wrong. "It's about Damon," she replied. "He was so proud that I noticed his shirt, he hasn't changed it all week! He's beginning to smell, and the other kids hold their noses when he comes into the room. Now what do I do?"

Greetings can be just as effective with older students, although they may not let us know how much they appreciate our attention.

At my suggestion, Mr. Lambeth started using farewells with his eighth graders. After a week with no student feedback, he complained that the technique wasn't working. I suggested that he stop for a few days and see what happened. Sure enough, the day he ceased saying goodbye, Sherice, a student in his first-period class, stopped by to ask him why he was mad at everyone. When he assured her he wasn't angry, she replied, "Then why didn't you stand at the door and say goodbye to us like you usually do?"

Like our students, we also feel the void created by the lack of A's in our lives.

Listen to Students

Perhaps the most powerful way to give attention is to listen when students have something on their mind they want to talk about. The topics may range from classroom concerns to problems with peers to family troubles. Listening to students requires more time than quick greetings, but even one fifteen-minute session can cement the teacher-student connection for the entire year.

Many teachers have difficulty listening to students talk about their problems. This discomfort stems from an incorrect belief that we must solve all the problems that students bring to us. The role of the teacher who listens is simply to provide a sympathetic ear. When we use good listening skills, we can help students talk through their concerns, and we can encourage them to create solutions. Good listening is a skill that everyone can develop. Here are some of the basics:

Keep quiet. When we don't know what to say, saying nothing is probably best. When we do know what to say, we need to be careful not to say it prematurely. We should interrupt only when absolutely necessary, such as when we need to slow down the student so we can understand what's being said.

Show interest with nonverbal signals. Make eye contact. Lean toward the student. Give an occasional nod. Mirror the student's nonverbal behavior by assuming a similar physical posture. This congruence of behavior sometimes helps the student feel comfortable with us.

NOT EVEN A SMILE—SO MUCH FOR BEING GOOD. FROM HERE ON IT'S NO MORE MR. NICE GIRL!

We need to "catch them being good" if we want to foster positive behavior choices.

Verbalize interest without words. Use encouraging sounds such as "Uh-huh" or "Mmmm," while keeping tone of voice and body language friendly.

Reflect back what the student has said. By paraphrasing in our own words what we think we've heard, we tell the student we're on the same wavelength. If we've misinterpreted, the student will correct us.

Ask questions sparingly. Use questions only to draw out more information, to clarify what's been said, or to help the student see possible solutions to the problem.

Seek out the student's feelings. The student's feeling is the real communication. We can ask about feelings directly: "How do you feel about that?" We can make a tentative guess and let the student correct us if we're wrong. We need to remind the student that all feelings are okay, even those that are powerful and upsetting. Sometimes we need to help the student distinguish feelings, which are all acceptable, from actions, which are not all acceptable.

Teach Students to Ask for Attention Wouldn't it be wonderful if students were willing to ask us for attention rather than misbehaving to get our attention? Even though we're not always able to provide attention at the precise moment students feel the need, we can promise that our attention will be available in the near future. We can keep a datebook or sign-up sheet for students who want to request an "attention date." Once students know when we'll be able to give them special attention, they usually are satisfied to wait.

A Potpourri of Ideas for Giving Attention

During inservice workshops, I've asked teachers how they pay special attention to students. Here are some of their ideas:

- Spend time chatting with students in the hall after class.
- Ask students about their life outside of the classroom.
- Remember what students talk to you about and mention these things when appropriate.
- Eat in the cafeteria with the students occasionally.
- Invite students, a few at a time, to eat lunch with you in your room.
- Attend school athletic, musical, and theatrical events.
- Get involved in a community project with your students.
- Schedule individual conferences with students.
- Join the students on the playground occasionally.
- Chaperon school events once in a while.
- Recognize birthdays in some way.
- Make bulletin boards with the students' baby pictures.
- Send cards, messages, and homework to absent students.
- Express real interest in students' work or hobbies.

Appreciation

To show students that we appreciate them, we can state how something they've done has benefited us, the class, or the school. Appreciation differs from applause in that the focus is on the contribution made rather than just on the act or accomplishment. Our appreciation needs to be spoken loudly and displayed clearly, for as Mark Twain put it, "The compliment that helps us on our way is not the one that is shut up in the mind, but the one that is spoken out."

Appreciate the Deed, Not the Doer Used correctly, appreciation is a powerful tool. Its misuse, however, may have harmful effects. Many of us have praised our students to the heavens and then watched their behavior deteriorate in minutes. The deterioration does not stem from the appreciation itself but from the manner in which it has been given. Appreciation is bestowed incorrectly when it addresses the *doer* in subjective terms: "What a good kid you are!" Judgmental words and evaluative statements—even positive ones—become the catalyst that often causes misbehavior to follow.

By focusing on the *deed*, we attach praise to the behavior that we wish to see continued: "Thank you for helping collect the papers." The student then knows exactly what she or he has done to gain our appreciation, which increases the chance that the student will repeat the same or similar behavior. Here are techniques necessary for effective use of appreciation:

Describe the behavior accurately. To show appreciation of a student's deeds, we need to pinpoint and describe behavior accurately. The same test for objectivity that we use to describe misbehavior can be applied to good behavior: Can our description of good behavior be documented by a video camera? Statements such as "Keep up the good work" or "Thanks for helping out" do not pass the documentary test. These general platitudes do not tell students exactly what they have done to earn the praise and, consequently, are not particularly effective in helping students continue to choose good behavior.

Use three-part appreciation statements. Once we have pinpointed the behavior, we can state our appreciation for it in the form of a three-part statement that describes the *student's action*, how *we feel* about the action, and the action's *positive effect*:

- "Anthony, when you clean up the science lab, I feel delighted, because it saves me time."
- "Nikia, when you complete your reading assignments on time like you did today, I feel great, because then the whole class can stay on schedule."

> *"The deepest principle of human nature is the craving to be appreciated."*
> —William James

Let students share their happygrams with you or each other.

When we give appreciation statements, we help students recognize the specific beneficial effects of their actions, which encourages them to keep behaving positively.

Focus only on the present. Appreciation statements are best received when they focus on the present moment. Saying "Anthony, how come you never cleaned the science lab before?" will only make Anthony feel discouraged about his past failings instead of proud of his present achievement. Similarly, any statement of future expectations can scare the student away. If we say, "Anthony, now I expect that every Friday afternoon you'll clean the science lab as well as you did today," Anthony is likely to be sorry he ever swabbed a test tube. Our appreciation statements need to remain free of comparisons or criticisms related to other behaviors.

Give Written Words of Appreciation Appreciation can be written as well as verbal. Students have been known to cherish notes of appreciation from teachers for great lengths of time. I'll never forget being told by a parent that her daughter had tacked above her desk in the college dorm an appreciation note I'd written her years ago.

We can write words of appreciation directly on students' papers, use happygrams, or even send E-mail messages via the "information superhighway."

Teach Students to Ask for Appreciation Since we can't see and comment on every positive thing that happens in the classroom, we can ask students to let us know when they deserve appreciation. Try this experiment: Put a box of assorted happygrams in the back of the room and invite students to write notes of appreciation to themselves about their own behavior. At the end of the day, have them read their notes to you. If you think the notes are accurate, sign them and encourage students to take them home.

This activity is a great exercise in building self-esteem because it enables students to learn how to appreciate themselves by noticing their own positive behavior.

Affirmation

To acknowledge a student's positive personality traits, we can make a verbal or written affirmation statement. Since traits are intangible and cannot be captured on film, they are best recognized via statements about the doer rather than the deed. Affirmation statements encourage students to believe in their known desirable traits and to become aware of hidden traits. When their positive traits are recognized, students feel good not only about themselves but also about us because we took the time to notice and comment.

The more vivid, specific, and enthusiastic our language, the greater the impact of our affirmation statement on a student. Here are some positive traits that we can acknowledge verbally or in writing:

ambition	fairness	patience
bravery	friendliness	persistence
cheerfulness	gentleness	politeness
cleanliness	good intentions	popularity
cleverness	graciousness	punctuality
consideration	helpfulness	risk-taking
courage	honesty	sensitivity
creativity	humility	seriousness
curiosity	intelligence	strength
dedication	kindness	talent
dependability	loyalty	thoughtfulness
effort	neatness	truthfulness
energy	organization	understanding
enthusiasm	originality	wit

Be a Talent Scout Think of yourself as a talent scout. *Every* student—including students with serious behavior problems or special needs—has at least one (and probably many) of the traits on this list. The time spent scouting around to find these talents will be paid back as the encouraged student makes responsible choices.

Making such statements as "I acknowledge your kindness" or "Wow! What creativity!" may seem strange at first. But once we see the wonderful effect of such statements on our students, we will quickly begin using them naturally. Most older children and adolescents respond best when we avoid loud, public announcements. A quiet voice, just loud enough for a few others to hear, is very effective.

Affection

In *The Whole Child*, Joanne Hendrick says, "An aura of happiness and affection . . . [establishes] that basic feeling of well-being which is essential to successful learning."[2] Good teachers are those who can not only present information in a coherent, intelligent manner but also establish mutually affectionate and rewarding relationships with their students.

Affection is a gift with no strings attached.

Affection Breeds Affection Affection is not a tool to be used to induce or reinforce a particular behavior. Rather, it is a gift with no strings attached. It is not "I like you when" or "I'd like you if." Instead, it is simply "I like you because I like you!"

Affection is always addressed to the doer, regardless of the deed. The message that each student needs to receive is this: "I'm likable no matter what. My teacher won't stop liking me if I make a mistake or get into trouble. My teacher likes me because I'm me!"

Affection is often most needed when things go badly. For example, consider this teacher's comments to a student who has failed a test: "Moya, I guess this last test just didn't go well for you. We all make mistakes, though, and maybe the next test will go better. Why don't we have lunch together today so we can talk some more?"

Such comments go a long way toward establishing a rewarding friendship with the student. Had the teacher pointed out to Moya that her inattention during lectures probably caused her to fail the test, Moya probably would have responded with resentment, and the situation might have worsened. The teacher's act of kindness—the lunch invitation—helps Moya understand that the teacher really respects her and cares about her.

Acts of kindness toward students can multiply astronomically:

> *A colleague of mine used to draw out students in a pensive mood by handing them a penny and saying, "Penny for your thoughts." One day, one of her students came to her and poured out an enormous pile of pennies collected from classmates. Looking up at her earnestly, the student explained, "We didn't want you to run out!"*

Students are more willing to follow the rules of a friend than a foe.

"What goes around, comes around," the saying goes. This is certainly true of affection. Those who demonstrate that they genuinely like us are hard to resist. Friendships with our students are some of our best assets when we have to discipline. Students are more willing to follow the rules and advice of a friend than those of a foe.

The Affectionate Touch
The value of touch has been well established. We've long known that infants thrive when they are touched and held frequently. This need to be touched stays with most of us all our lives, which makes handshakes, back pats, and hugs very effective ways to show affection.

Valid concerns do exist about the amount and kind of touching appropriate in a school setting. The best guideline is the comfort level of both the teacher and the student; for older students, the side-by-side, one-arm hug works well. Of particular importance is using common sense and sensitivity in regard to touching all students, especially those in middle school and junior and senior high. Young people at these ages are not always in control of their sexual feelings, and a nurturing hug could easily be misconstrued. It's best to do all our affectionate touching in open environments, with the door to our classroom and the shades or drapes open.

We also have to take into account that students who have a lot of power and revenge behaviors generally do not like to be touched by teachers. With these students, we have to stick to verbal forms of affection.

How Many A's Make an A+ Relationship?

Teachers often ask if overdoing the A's won't result in "spoiled students." Can we give too much attention? express too much appreciation? show too much affection? I don't think we ever could spoil students with too many A's; we do, however, "spoil" students in three other ways:

- when we overlook their misbehaviors and don't take appropriate action
- when we do too many things for them that they could do for themselves
- when we bail them out of unpleasant situations that they themselves created

When given appropriately, the A's are always helpful. In fact, we could double, triple, even quadruple the dosage without risking harmful side effects!

A's for Students Who Are Hard to Help One disheartening thing about the A's is that they are difficult to give to those students who need them most. Who feels like appreciating a student who causes no end of trouble day after day? However difficult this may be for us, acting positively toward such a student is crucial to his or her well-being. Once we begin, we'll find it becomes easier and easier to continue, and we'll discover that our boosts to the student's self-esteem will pay off in improved behavior.

A's for Students Who Don't Hear Us Another point to keep in mind about giving A's is that many young people don't hear positive remarks. They're so used to being criticized and reprimanded that kind words just pass by them. We may need to watch a student's facial expression and body language to make sure we've made an impression. If we haven't, we'll have to repeat what we've said or even ask, "Did you hear what I just said?" Sometimes we have to teach students to be receptive to an A+ relationship. Once they begin experiencing the benefits of this new way of relating, however, they will soon become eager participants.

A's to Help Students Cope With Stress Childhood can't always be happy. All the ills of society that put stress on us also stress our students. We have to be careful not to fall into the trap of excusing irresponsible behavior because of these stressful circumstances. But we can be compassionate.

We must not fall into the trap of excusing irresponsible behavior because of stressful circumstances.

Increasing the A's is the best response when we perceive that a student is experiencing stress. Whatever the cause of the stress—an illness, a breakup with a girlfriend or boyfriend, a difficult family situation—we can immediately respond by upping the student's intake of "vitamin A's." At the same time we can hold students accountable for their behavior, using the interventions for attention, power, revenge, and avoidance-of-failure that we've already explored.

A's and Gang Prevention   When gang members are interviewed by the press or by researchers, one theme stands out: that being in a gang is a way of connecting. "The gang is my family." "I joined because no one else cares about me." "It's the only place I really belong." What's being expressed is the need for affiliation—the need to feel wanted, to belong. Think about how well gang members connect through the use of colors, clothes, handshakes, verbal signals, graffiti, and gang-sanctioned antisocial behaviors.

One of our best prevention weapons to defeat gang formation is to beat them at their own game. We can use the strategies to connect, teacher-to-student. We can promote these strategies student-to-student by encouraging students to use the A's among themselves. The goals are to satisfy the need for affiliation in the classroom and in the school and to begin to undermine at least one motivation for joining gangs.

Notes

1. Barbara Clark, *Growing Up Gifted* (Columbus, OH: Merrill, 1979), 154.
2. Joanne Hendrick, *The Whole Child: New Trends in Early Education* (St. Louis: Mosby, 1980), 4.

A s teachers, we want to encourage students to care about and contribute to their class, their school, and their community. When
we help students understand that their personal welfare is linked to
the welfare of others, we are well on the way to developing responsible, concerned, and involved citizens.

"The need to be needed is often more powerful than the need to
survive," states Dr. Stephen Glenn in *Raising Children for Success*.[1]
Glenn hypothesizes that depression and suicide result from the perception that one's life has no meaning, no purpose, no significance.
When we structure our rooms so that each student is asked to contribute to the welfare of the class, school, and community, we satisfy
the need to be needed in at least one area of a young person's life.

When students contribute, they feel needed. Students who are
needed feel they belong. Those who belong develop high self-esteem.
Students with high self-esteem have much to contribute. It's a wonderful circular process in which each part reinforces the others.

When we invite students to contribute, we send the message that
we believe they have something of value to give to others. This powerful message strengthens our relationship to them and builds the connection that proves we care. When they know we care, they care.
Another wonderful circular process takes place in which each part
reinforces the other.

Satisfying the Need to Be Needed

We can encourage students to contribute by using the techniques
described in this chapter, which are grouped according to five strategies. Encourage student input into creating additional techniques for
applying these strategies. Rotate student involvement when special
helpers are appointed and committees are formed so that all students
have a chance to participate in as many ways as possible.

*Make a special effort
to help students with
avoidance-of-failure
behaviors and
disabilities feel
needed.*

Strategy 1: Encourage Students' Contributions to the Class

When we give students some responsibility as well as voice and
choice in classroom and curriculum matters, we foster critical thinking skills, inspire a sense of ownership, and promote an attitude of
willing participation. Asking students to state opinions and preferences
involves granting them a certain amount of independence and legitimate power. We've already learned that allowing legitimate power is

an essential precaution against the eruption of power struggles in the classroom.

Involve Students in Building the Learning Environment

When students are involved in creating and maintaining a stimulating learning environment in the classroom, they have the opportunity to contribute to the welfare of the classroom and to learn valuable skills at the same time. And while they are selecting titles for a collection of books on life in Revolutionary times, creating a bulletin board collage of Asian cities, or scavenging scraps for an arts-and-crafts corner, the time we would have spent performing these tasks can be spent helping and encouraging those in need of our assistance.

Inviting students to contribute sends the message that we believe they have something of value to give to others.

Invite Students' Help With Daily Tasks
Another way to enable students to contribute to the welfare of the class is to turn over to them as many of the daily classroom duties as possible. So many of the tasks we spend time on don't require our expertise. For example, students can take attendance, inventory books and supplies, deliver messages, collect lunch money, straighten up, sort worksheets, alphabetize books, and operate audiovisual equipment.

Students enjoy helping out. They relish being useful. As long as we demonstrate the attitude that "I'm asking you to do this because I know you are capable and I need your help," students see tasks as privileges instead of chores. On the other hand, if we give the impression that we're asking for their help because the task is too menial for us, they'll refuse.

When making out the beginning-of-the-year task chart, one wise middle school teacher always lists two or three more tasks than there are students in her class. That way there are tasks for students entering class later in the year. You can bet that a new student feels instantly connected and valued in her classroom.

Request Students' Curriculum Choices
Inviting students to express their opinions and preferences concerning the curriculum is especially effective in secondary schools. Often we can present students with choices about when, how, and even where a certain subject or lesson is conducted. Consider this example:

The tenth-grade English curriculum at Harbor High calls for students to read one of Shakespeare's plays. Students in Mr. Nguyen's class chose to read the play before spring break, while students in Ms. Peltham's class decided to begin after the break. Mr. Nguyen's students opted to assign parts and read the play aloud, while Ms. Peltham's wanted to use various video and audio recordings. Mr Nguyen's class chose to write one long paper, while Ms. Peltham's students decided to write several short essays.

Allowing students this kind of autonomy gives them a vested interest in actively participating in the class, and it may give us a fresh perspective on material we've been teaching for years. Older students can also choose learning goals, write learning contracts, decide which resources to use, and carry out in-depth courses of study quite independently.

Even first graders can make some simple curriculum and procedural choices: Should we sit around a table during reading time, or should we sit in a circle on a rug in the corner of the room? Should we record each person reading a sentence out loud? How should our worksheets be done today, in pencil or crayon?

Designate Class Liaisons Individual students can be given the responsibility to bring announcements and messages from various staff members to the class. Would the school librarian like everyone to know that the latest issues of *Sports Illustrated* and *Seventeen* have arrived? Does the principal want students to be aware of a special assembly to be held next week? Perhaps the lunchroom staff wants students to know that there's a change in tomorrow's menu. The students who act as liaisons not only contribute to the welfare of the class, they also enhance their relationship with other adults in the building.

Appoint Reporters Are problems developing in the cafeteria, on the playground, aboard the school bus? The job of the reporter is to be aware when problems occur in these areas and to bring the problems to a class discussion or class meeting where solutions can be devised.

Delegate Responsibility for Specific Functions The supply manager makes sure that the everyday supply needs such as chalk and paper are looked after. The class meeting chairperson schedules the meetings and plans the agenda. The current-affairs coordinator sees that local news is posted daily on the bulletin board. Invite your students to create positions they feel would improve the functioning of the class.

Strategy 2: Encourage Students' Contributions to the School

I consider the strategies in this section and the three that follow as citizenship training. Students who have been encouraged to contribute to the school, the community, and the environment are learning first-hand that they play an important role in creating a safe, orderly, and caring environment.

Appoint Area Monitors Crossing guards, playground patrols, hall monitors, and lunchroom leaders all have the function of assisting with the operation of the area to which they are assigned, under the direction of the appropriate staff member.

Create a Three C Committee Creating a community of learners built on high self-esteem is the task of the Three C committee. Committee members use their creativity to apply the strategies for feeling capable, connecting, and contributing to all areas and people within the school. Many schools include students, staff, and parents as members of this committee.

Schedule Work Service Periods When I was in high school, every Friday afternoon from 2:00 until 3:30 was work service time. During this hour and a half students performed such services as raking leaves, dusting library shelves, and scrubbing cafeteria tables. Would we rather have been practicing cheerleading, completing assignments, or simply schmoozing with our friends during that time? Of course. Yet we felt pride in how good the school looked on Monday mornings. And we were more careful about not messing up the building or the grounds than we probably would have been if our labor had not been required to help clean up the messes.

Establish a Crime Watch Patrol To decrease the amount of violence and illegal behaviors in today's schools, a partnership can be established with local law enforcement agencies. The students on the crime watch patrol assume the responsibility for reporting any signs of illegal or potentially dangerous behaviors. While one might fear some students would perceive this patrol as "snitching," this fear seems to be largely unfounded. Most young people want to feel safe at school. They are as concerned as teachers about ridding their schools of criminal activity.

Strategy 3: Encourage Students' Contributions to the Community

When we encourage students to contribute to the welfare of the surrounding community, we foster attitudes and behaviors that have a good chance of blossoming into lifelong commitments to generosity, altruism, and service.

Students who've been encouraged to contribute are learning good citizenship.

Adopt a Health Care Center Residents of health care centers enjoy listening to students read, sing, play instruments, and put on skits. They also appreciate students who are willing to write letters for them and perform simple errands. Students benefit not only from the satisfaction of being able to make a contribution, but also from listening to older folks describe the long-ago world of their youth and from seeing people with physical barriers work to regain living skills.

Adopt a Zoo Animal Here in Tampa, where I live, each zoo animal is put up for adoption. The adopting "parents" provide money for the animal's upkeep and stay abreast of the progress of their "child." When a whole class adopts an animal, students perform fund-raising activities to cover the costs of the adoption. The students, of course, are motivated to research everything they can about their adopted animal, such as food requirements, native habitat, and mating rituals.

Contribute to Community Drives Most communities sponsor food drives, Meals on Wheels, Toys for Tots, and disaster relief and other drives. Participating in these community actions helps students become sensitive to the needs of others. We can also consider the whole world our community and involve students in projects to help children, families, and schools around the globe.

Promote Volunteerism Individual students may choose to volunteer at local institutions. When we ask them to report back to the class about the services they are providing, these students become models other students may choose to follow.

Every cause affords students many learning opportunities as well as the ability to contribute.

Acknowledge Random Acts of Kindness Each day offers us all opportunities to help others: Carrying packages in the mall parking lot for a mother trying to manage bundles as well as two squirming toddlers. Saying "How nice you're able to be back with us" to the man who has returned to church after a hospital stay. The more we encourage students to talk about random acts of kindness they see or do, the more such acts will occur.

Strategy 4: Encourage Students to Work to Protect the Environment

Mother Earth needs the help of all our students. Your class may want to join and support a cause such as saving the whales or preserving a wilderness area. Every cause affords students the opportunity to do research, read, debate, and write to Congress as they search for solutions to problems in the environment.

Take Part in Recycling and Antilitter Campaigns In many areas, groups of people "adopt" streets or part of a roadway and assume the responsibility for keeping the area litter free. My hunch is that after picking up other people's trash, students will be less likely to toss an empty pop can or candy wrapper on the ground.

Strategy 5: Encourage Students to Help Other Students

When students help one another, their self-esteem rises. They are able not only to make a significant contribution to the class but also to establish a special connection with classmates.

Circle of Friends Renae Porter, a middle school teacher in the Seattle area, developed a program she calls "Circle of Friends":

When her district moved toward a policy of inclusion of special-needs students into the regular classroom, she noticed that many of the children involved were friendless and excluded from the "in" groups. She worked with students who became a Circle of Friends, whose mission was to take new students under their wing and help them satisfy their need to belong. The friends made sure that each student had a partner to sit with during lunch, had someone to walk and talk with between classes, and was invited to join activities with other classmates.

For students who fear failure, nonacademic tutoring provides a taste of success.

Peer Tutoring Tutoring is one way in which students can help each other. If a student is having trouble with a geometry theorem that we've just explained for the third time, chances are that another student's explanation will make more sense than our fourth try. A struggling student's anxiety level is often lessened when a peer presents the information. Students do seem to speak a special language of their own, often unknown to the teacher. In any class, we can usually find many potential "pupil professors" who are willing to assist classmates.[2]

Peer tutoring helps the tutor as much as the tutee. When Ali has to explain the use of coordinates on a map to another child, he must first clarify his own understanding and perfect his own skills.

Students whose first language is not English benefit greatly from peers who can help them with language acquisition and with learning the prescribed curriculum.

Students in every grade can get involved in peer tutoring. Seventh graders can help other seventh graders with social studies, or fifth graders can help first graders with reading skills. High school math whizzes can help students at all grade levels with math. I've even seen eight-year-old "computerniks" show high schoolers how to write simple programs. And every student is capable of making a contribution when peer tutoring occurs in nonacademic areas:

I remember Marcia, a sixth grader at least three years behind in basic skills, who volunteered to teach jumping rope. First graders with poor motor coordination thoroughly enjoyed working with Marcia to master this skill. In turn, Marcia's self-esteem was enhanced.

Peer Counseling Another way that students can contribute to the welfare of classmates is through adult-supervised peer counseling programs. Many secondary schools have established such programs in which students work with peers experiencing difficulty in some aspect of their life. Peer counseling is done one-to-one or in small groups.

As with peer tutoring, peer counseling helps the counselor as much as the counselee. The training that student counselors receive in communication skills and in personal development issues is invaluable. The experience of being able to help a classmate overcome a difficulty also provides a real boost to self-esteem.

Peer Mediation In an effort to decrease the growing amount of conflict between and among students, many schools are establishing peer mediation programs that train selected students in a step-by-step process to mediate disputes.

Peer Recognition Another way we can enable students to help one another is through peer recognition activities. These are several effective techniques:

- Applause—We can encourage students to applaud one another's achievements.
- Appreciation and Affirmation Statements—We can teach students how to make effective appreciation statements to one another and how to affirm one another's positive traits.
- Happygrams—Students can write happygrams to one another that contain appreciation statements. In schools with modern technology, students can send a "fantastic fax" or "excellent E-mail."
- Appreciation Password—Each student can be asked to say a few words of appreciation to another student before leaving the room for lunch or another class.

Notes

1. H. Stephen Glenn and Jane Nelsen, *Raising Children for Success* (Fair Oaks, CA: Sunrise Press, 1987), 87.
2. A good resource to help institute peer helping in your classroom or school is Robert P. Bowman and John N. Chanaca, *Peer Pals: Kids Helping Kids Succeed in School* (Circle Pines, MN: American Guidance Service, 1994).

CHAPTER 16
The Classroom Code of Conduct

We've looked at using the encouragement process to help students gain a strong sense of belonging in our classrooms. Another important way to involve students and foster their sense of responsibility to the group is by working with them to develop a classroom code of conduct. By replacing teacher-dictated rules with a code of conduct developed through collaboration, we bring the concept of Cooperative Discipline full circle.

How Rules Work Against Us

When we rely on rules for managing and controlling student behavior, problems occur. The word *rule* itself causes difficulty, because students—especially secondary students—tend to perceive this four-letter word as "how adults control kids." Rules allow too much "wiggle room" for an articulate student to find loopholes and squirm through. After all, we can't have a rule to cover every situation that occurs in a school building. Even if we could, having too many rules creates a negative classroom environment that focuses on obedience rather than responsibility.

These pitfalls can be avoided when we replace most rules with a classroom code of conduct. A code of conduct defines the operating principles that govern the behavior of everyone in the class. It sets the standards for how everyone is expected to interact—including the teacher! With a code of conduct, all students are held accountable for *all* of their behavior all of the time.

Establishing a code of conduct doesn't preclude setting a minimum number of rules to cover specific situations, especially those involving safety. And if your school has a few schoolwide rules to be followed by all students, these can't be ignored.[1] You'll most likely find, however, that a well-defined code of conduct also covers the situations for which those rules are intended.

If it is to be effective, the code of conduct must apply to all.

A Code of Conduct for a Safe and Orderly Classroom

A well-developed code of conduct is encouragement in action. Everyone in the class is given the information they need to feel *capable* of choosing responsible behavior in *our* classroom. For students from a variety of cultures with different traditions regarding behavior, having this information is crucial to their success. Moreover, the process of defining and teaching the code promotes the *connection* between students as well as inviting them to *contribute* to the welfare of the class.

In addition to creating a positive and safe classroom environment, establishing a code provides a vehicle for putting into practice many of the principles we've discussed in previous chapters. The process of defining the code of conduct exemplifies the hands-joined management style, with students actively involved in setting the expectations and limits for their behavior. Asking parents for their input in defining and teaching the code of conduct promotes cooperation between home and school.

Teachers who have developed a code of conduct report a significant decrease in power struggles in the classroom. This fortuitous phenomenon occurs because students are allowed voice and choice and are granted legitimate power in the process of creating and maintaining the code.

Perhaps the code of conduct's greatest benefit for us busy teachers is that the responsibility for monitoring behavior no longer rests solely on our shoulders. Instead, this responsibility becomes shared with students, who learn to evaluate their own behavioral decisions on a moment-to-moment basis.

Defining the Code of Conduct

In my ideal classroom, students would treat each other with courtesy, show respect for school and personal property, be diligent about their learning, and do everything in their power to maintain a positive, safe, and encouraging learning environment.

Envision the Ideal If you could envision your ideal classroom, what would it look and sound like? How would the students behave toward you, toward each other, toward their learning? Our vision of the ideal tells us where we want our code of conduct to take us. Once we know the destination, we can identify the operating principles—defined as statements of behavioral expectations—that will get us there.

Ask Students for Their Vision Students at all levels need to be involved in the process of defining the code of conduct. Through discussions and class meetings, they can define what their ideal classroom would be like. Most teachers find it simple to merge their vision with their students', because students tend to want the same kind of classroom we do. They're as much bothered by disruptive and irresponsible behavior on the part of their peers as we are.

Ask Parents for Their Vision Parental involvement at this stage is also desirable. Involve parents by sending them a letter summarizing the ideas students express and asking for comments and suggestions. Or during open school night, invite parents to describe the ideal classroom they'd like for their children.

Operating Principles: Four Examples

Once we know what we, our students, and parents want, we take the vision and identify the operating principles needed to achieve it. Consider the following collaborative codes of conduct.

A code of conduct brings together members of the class and sets a high standard for responsible behavior.

From Big Springs Elementary School in Richardson, Texas:

I am respectful.
I am responsible.
I am safe.
I am prepared.

We are here to learn. Therefore I will:

• Respect myself, others, and the environment.
• Cooperate with all school people.
• Do nothing to keep the teacher from teaching and anyone, myself included, from learning.

The same code of conduct, revised for a secondary classroom:

I am respectful.
I am responsible.
I am safe.
I am prepared.

Because "Excellence in Education" is our motto, I will:

• Do nothing to prevent the teacher from teaching and anyone, myself included, from participating in educational endeavors.
• Cooperate with all members of the school community.
• Respect myself, others, and the environment.

From Explorer Middle School in Everett, Washington:

The entire school community is positively and actively involved with one another. Everyone in the Explorer Community is entitled to feel positive, safe, and cared about. Therefore, I will:

• Treat everyone with courtesy and respect.
• Help create and maintain a safe and positive learning environment.
• Show respect for school and personal property.

1. I will treat everyone with courtesy and respect.

2. I will treat personal and school property with respect.

3. I will help create and maintain a positive and safe environment.

4. I will come to school prepared for learning.

5. I will act responsibly and accept consequences for my actions.

6. I will help everyone in this school feel capable, connected, and contributing.

As you can see, the operating principles that make up the code of conduct differ from rules in a number of significant ways. Notice how general and global the statements are. And how personal. It's hard to think of a classroom situation for which at least one of these operating principles would not apply.

Notice also that the principles are written in terms of "I." "I am" or "I will" statements emphasize each person's commitment and responsibility to follow the code. Many codes include references to the Three Cs, which are the building blocks of self-esteem.

Teaching the Code of Conduct

Three steps are needed to teach the code of conduct.

1. Identify Appropriate and Inappropriate Behaviors

Begin by conducting a discussion in which you ask students to identify specific behaviors that are appropriate and inappropriate to each operating principle. The list of specific behaviors generated will make the code of conduct understandable and relevant to each student.

For example, an eighth-grade class discussing the operating principle "I will treat everyone with courtesy and respect" might list these *appropriate* behaviors:

• Call people by their given name.
• Use a pleasant tone of voice.
• Keep my hands to myself.
• Listen when others are speaking.
• Use proper language at all times.
• Respond politely to requests from teachers and classmates.

Some of the behaviors these eighth graders might list as *inappropriate* to the principle might be:

- obscene gestures
- put-downs
- name-calling
- pushing and shoving
- ridiculing
- remarks that reflect cultural stereotypes
- ethnic jokes

The operating principle "I will treat everyone with courtesy and respect" could apply to all grades K-12. The list of appropriate and inappropriate behaviors and the words students use to describe them will vary depending on grade level. The goal of this identification process is for every student in the class, regardless of age, ability level, or background, to be clear about which behaviors are appropriate and which are not.

It doesn't matter if these lists become lengthy. No one has to memorize them. Rather, the purpose of generating the lists is to help students sharpen their powers of evaluation and judgment and understand that they will be held accountable for *all* of their behaviors *all* of the time.

Save the lists of appropriate and inappropriate behaviors. Add to them as necessary and review them periodically, particularly after long vacations or when student behavior indicates that a principle needs to be reexamined.

2. Clarify Appropriate and Inappropriate Behaviors
It is crucial that every student have a clear idea of what each of the identified behaviors actually is. Otherwise, arguments may occur about whether a given behavior is or isn't appropriate.

To clarify attributes and characteristics of each identified behavior, model or have students model the listed behaviors. Or have students role-play specific situations that portray the behaviors. Or have students draw scenes or write stories about situations involving the behaviors.

Another good way to clarify is by having students use their thespian talents. For example, students might role-play the difference between addressing someone in pleasant tones and unpleasant tones. In one middle school, a single operating principle was assigned to five classes. Each class's task was to devise a skit concerning behaviors relating to the assigned principle and to present the skit during a school assembly.

3. Involve Parents
Most parents want to be involved and can do a lot toward helping teach the code of conduct. Students could individually or collectively write a letter to parents that explains the code of conduct and lists the corresponding appropriate and inappropriate behaviors. Add a postscript asking parents to save and use the letter as a springboard for discussions with their children about the behaviors they're choosing in school.

Every student in the class needs to be clear about which behaviors are acceptable and which are not.

Enforcing the Code of Conduct

Consistency in enforcing the code of conduct is crucial. Three steps are involved in accomplishing this task.

1. Check for Understanding We can ask misbehaving students questions to ensure that they grasp the inappropriateness of their behavior as it relates to the code. Any of these questions check for understanding:

- "What behavior are you choosing at this moment?"
- "Is the behavior you're choosing right now appropriate to our code of conduct?"
- "Which part of our code of conduct does this behavior relate to?"
- "Is this behavior on our *appropriate* or *inappropriate* list of behaviors?"
- "Given our class code of conduct, what should I say to you right now?"
- "Can you help me understand why you are violating our code of conduct at this moment?"

When using any of these questions, be sure to assume a businesslike manner, with no accusatory overtones. All of the emergency preparedness techniques discussed in Chapter 9 are applicable in this situation.

2. Problem-Solve When Disagreements Occur At times, students may disagree with us about the appropriateness or inappropriateness of a specific behavior. We can resolve these disagreements in one of three ways:

- with a student-teacher conference, involving parents, counselors, and administrators where necessary
- in a class meeting that focuses on evaluating the behavior, not the student
- by any mediation or conflict resolution process

The last four chapters of this book discuss cooperative conflict resolution and a detailed Action Plan Process we can use to deal with recurring misbehavior.

3. Post the Code of Conduct Many teachers like to keep their classroom code of conduct posted as a reminder about how everyone in the classroom is expected to behave. Another benefit of posting the code is that it can be used as an intervention technique when a student chooses inappropriate behavior.

Here are some ways teachers have found effective for using the posted code of conduct:

- Walk over to the code of conduct, point to the operating principle that is being violated, and make eye contact with the misbehaving student. If eye contact isn't enough, use attention interventions such as name dropping, a secret signal, or standing close by (Chapter 5).
- Write the number of the code being broken, or a word from it, on a self-stick note and put it on the student's desk.
- Point to the operating principle being violated and say, "Read number 3, please, Thesa." When many students are misbehaving at the same time, this statement becomes "Class, read principle number 3, please."
- Point to the operating principle being violated and say, "Tell me in your own words what this means, Raul" or, "Arianna, is there something you don't understand about this part of our code of conduct?"

Of course, we can use any of the intervention strategies for attention, power, revenge, and avoidance-of-failure when a student violates the code of conduct.

Reinforcing the Code of Conduct

As with all skills, periodic reinforcement is required if we want students to become proficient at monitoring and evaluating their own behavior.

Publicize the Code of Conduct The more they see it, the more students are reminded of the expectations for their behavior. Some ways to publicize the code include:

Double standards do not help us build a cooperative spirit in the classroom.

- displaying student-designed posters illustrating the code
- printing the code on a form for all students and their parents to read, sign, and return
- reciting the code daily after the Pledge of Allegiance or morning announcements

Model Self-Correction If students are to learn how to self-correct inappropriate behavior without losing face, they need to observe teachers doing this. Publicly holding ourselves accountable sends a powerful message to students:

> *During the last period of the day, Mrs. Bielka found herself yelling at her whole class of sixth graders instead of dealing quietly with the three students in the back of the room who were off-task. The next day, she told the class, "I'm sorry I yelled at all of you yesterday. My behavior certainly violated the part of the code that talks about showing respect. Here's what I'll do differently if I'm faced with the same situation again."*

Encourage Student Evaluation We can help students grow in their progress and ability to choose appropriate behavior by encouraging self-evaluation. We might ask students to write a list of specific behaviors they are choosing that exemplify the code of conduct. Save the lists so students can compare them over a period of time to assess progress. Or post the lists, read them aloud, or send them home to parents. Positive self-evaluation and self-applause are powerful motivators for students' continued efforts at improved behavior.

An extension of self-evaluation might be a goal-setting activity. Using a scale of 1-5, students can rate their adherence to each operating principle and then decide what they can do to raise their position on the scale. Help students determine a reasonable time frame to accomplish this kind of change. Sharing their goals in small groups provides opportunities for students to exchange ideas on how to achieve their goals and support each other.

Notes

1. Detailed instructions for creating a *schoolwide* code of conduct are found in Linda Albert, *An Administrator's Guide to Cooperative Discipline* (Circle Pines, MN: American Guidance Service, 1992), 83-94.
2. For information about *Cooperative Discipline: The Graduate Course*, call AGS at 1-800-328-2560.

CHAPTER 17
Cooperative Conflict Resolution

Open almost any catalog of educational materials and you'll surely find specialized programs in conflict resolution and peer mediation. Should this trend continue, "Resolving Conflicts"—along with reading, 'riting, and 'rithmetic—could easily become the fourth R in education. Unfortunately, many well-intentioned efforts at conflict resolution are doomed to failure because they're installed in classrooms and schools without the underlying structure of effective discipline built on caring relationships and mutual respect.

The most important prerequisite for effective conflict resolution is a Three C classroom, which establishes a class culture where we communicate to solve problems in a caring and respectful manner. Since all conflict resolution systems and procedures require the willingness of students to cooperate in the search for solutions, we cultivate this willingness by implementing the Three C strategies. Students who perceive that we care enough to help them feel capable, connected, and contributing usually reciprocate by caring enough to work with us to resolve conflicts.

Chapters 18-20 discuss using the Action Plan Process to work with students who repeatedly choose to misbehave for attention, power, revenge, or avoidance-of-failure. The procedures for cooperative conflict resolution can be used within that process. They are especially helpful when dealing with power and revenge behaviors. One of the graceful exits for intervening at the moment of misbehavior when these behaviors occur is to schedule a conference. The plan that results from this conference fulfills the resolution stage of dealing with classroom volcanoes.

The conflict resolution procedures can also be used independently, when you need to resolve a conflict with a student who does not constantly misbehave and is therefore not a candidate for a full action plan.

It's important for students to learn about conflict and how to handle it.

Setting the Tone for Teacher-Student Conflict Resolution

The attitude we bring to the conflict resolution conference sets the tone. If we want the student actively to engage in the search for solutions, we must be many things: empathic, nonaccusatory, encouraging, nonemotional, respectful, firm yet friendly, and fair.

Keeping in mind the student's needs will also help ensure the success of the conflict resolution process:

- To feel heard—"My teacher is willing to listen to me."
- To feel understood—"My teacher is willing to listen to how I feel and what I think I need without putting me down."
- To feel empowered—"I have control over myself and what I do. I can choose my behavior and my reactions to situations."
- To feel worthwhile—"I am not a bad person, and there is a place for me in this class."
- To have self-esteem left intact—"I am capable. I can find ways to connect and to contribute even though I misbehaved in the past."
- To be future oriented—"I can't undo the bad choice I've already made, but I can make a better choice next time."

Keeping the tone of the conference positive sends the message that the issue is the behavior, not the student personally. The teacher-student relationship is thereby strengthened, even though a serious problem is being discussed.

The Teacher-Student Conflict Resolution Conference

Conferences need to be win-win situations.

Resolving conflicts means finding solutions that are acceptable to both teacher and student. Cooperative Discipline uses a Six D process.

Step 1: Define the problem objectively. Objectively pinpoint and describe the behavior causing the problem.

Step 2: Declare the need. What is it that makes the identified behavior a problem for both teacher and student? Mutual understanding of needs often changes each person's perception of the problem and adds to the willingness to seek solutions.

Step 3: Describe the feelings. Once both the teacher's and the student's feelings are expressed, the way is paved for a rational, rather than emotional, handling of the problem.

Step 4: Discuss solutions. Consider several solutions to the problem. Use brainstorming to generate as many alternatives as possible. Evaluate the pros and cons as each suggestion is discussed or after the brainstorming is finished.

Step 5: Decide on a plan. To do this, choose the solution with the most pros from both points of view. Be specific about when the plan will begin; set the date when the plan's effectiveness will be evaluated. Many teachers like the agreed-upon plan to be written and signed by both student and teacher.

Students' perceptions of the teacher's attitude will affect how they approach conflict resolution.

Step 6: Determine the plan's effectiveness. Meet with the student on the specified date. If either person's needs still are not being met, a new solution can be negotiated by repeating Steps 2-4.

Conflict Resolution With "Difficult" Students

Despite our best efforts, not every misbehaving student will be willing to negotiate with us in good faith. We can sidestep the following "blocking" behaviors by keeping our cool and using strategies that keep us in control of the conference.

Stonewalling When students stonewall, they refuse to respond verbally and negotiate with us. If there's no response after a couple of attempts, we can simply say, "Since you're not ready to talk about it, I'll decide what happens next." Wait a few seconds for a response. Because most students want to be part of the decision-making process, at this point they typically respond. If, however, the student continues to stonewall, we state what we plan to do next, thank the student for coming, and end the conference.

Unworkable Solutions Sometimes a student will give an unworkable solution, one that we feel is inappropriate. Our challenge is to reject the suggestion and still encourage the student's continued cooperation in negotiating. We can respond by saying, "I'm unwilling to try that because _____. Do you have another idea?" Conferences need to be win-win situations. With continued brainstorming, usually a mutually agreeable solution can be found.

Verbal Disrespect Some students will use words to anger and frustrate us and try to bring the conference to a halt. Many of the graceful exit techniques are appropriate when this happens. Another response is to offer a simple choice: "Your choice is to treat me with respect or be excused to the office. You decide."

Blaming Others How skillful students are in implicating everyone but themselves! We can respond with, "I hear you, but that's not the issue. I'm interested in finding a solution for the problem you and I are having."

Student-Student Conflict Resolution

Many formal student-student conflict resolution and peer mediation programs exist that are extremely effective schoolwide. In the classroom, however, the Six D process works as well student to student as it does teacher to student and is therefore a valuable part of schoolwide efforts to reduce conflict and potentially violent behavior. When resolving student-student conflicts, a helpful modification to the process is to have a student not involved in the conflict conduct the conference and lead the participants through the six steps.

Learning about conflict and how to handle it is important for all students. Therefore it's preferable to teach everyone in the class how to use these procedures rather than just a few who might serve as the "official" mediators. Programs that teach students how to avoid conflicts, thereby reducing violence and increasing everyone's personal safety, help establish a classroom climate based on peaceful cooperation.[1]

Note

1. Two excellent programs for conflict resolution and gang prevention are the Wilder Foundation's *Cool 2B Safe* (St. Paul: Wilder Foundation, 1995) and AGS Media's *Connection and Clear Limits*, program 1 in the series *Gangs and Group Violence* (Louisville: AGS Media, 1995).

CHAPTER 18
The School Action Plan Process

*F*or students whose misbehavior continues to be a problem, we have yet another powerful tool: the School Action Plan. We create the plan to guide our interactions with a student, with the goal being to influence change in the student's behavior. The plan represents our commitment to encouraging the student to make appropriate choices while trying to satisfy the ultimate need—to belong.

Designing a School Action Plan takes time, but a thoughtfully composed plan has payoffs that reward our efforts. Just the act of planning can relieve our stress and frustration. As we write about a student's misbehavior and plot a course of action, we usually come to the realization that effecting change is possible. Transferring our observations and thoughts to paper gives us a positive charge mentally. It removes uncertainty from the discipline process and replaces it with the expectation of success.

A Written School Action Plan

Most of the time, when misbehavior occurs, we'll proceed through the steps of the School Action Plan spontaneously. As we become skilled with the Cooperative Discipline procedures, we'll be able to identify the goal of misbehavior quickly and react appropriately, reminding ourselves that at a later time we'll need to use more encouragement strategies with this misbehaving student. We'll want to use a written School Action Plan when:

Designing a School Action Plan takes time, but its payoffs reward our efforts.

- The misbehavior continues or is consistently repeated over a period of time.
- Consequences, a conflict resolution conference, or both are part of the plan.
- We want to be able to communicate and collaborate with colleagues and parents in a mutually supportive manner.

School Action Plan Step 1: Pinpoint and Describe the Student's Behavior

Before we can help a student choose to stop misbehaving, we have to pinpoint and describe the behaviors that are causing us the most concern. We want to list only the three or four most troublesome behaviors, not every transgression the student has ever committed! Limiting this list may be frustrating when a student seems to have 537 miserable behaviors. Take heart! Each time we successfully redirect one behavior, we are chipping away at the student's perception that similar behaviors will satisfy the need to belong. By influencing a student's choices of how to satisfy this need, we'll be nurturing change in the student's overall behavior pattern.

The Key to Accuracy: Gather and State Facts

Just as newspaper reporters need to gather facts before they can write an accurate story, so we need to gather facts before we can describe a student's behavior objectively. A comprehensive description includes exactly *what* the student does to misbehave, *when* the student usually does it, and approximately *how often*.

Avoid Subjective Terms The *what* of misbehavior needs to be a straightforward statement with no subjective garnishes. Our natural tendency is to view misbehavior in terms of how it affects us or in relation to our expectations of how a student should behave. To achieve objectivity, we need to train ourselves to become impartial observers. For example, consider the inherent bias that marks each of these statements:

- "Jerrod is totally impossible. I don't know what to do with him."
- "Janna is so scattered. Pray you don't get her next year!"
- "Jason is so immature."
- "Julian is one of the most uncooperative kids I've ever had."
- "Jolinda is so disruptive. She drives me crazy!"

The descriptors used—*impossible, scattered, immature, uncooperative, disruptive*—affect teachers almost as negatively as the behaviors themselves. For example, by calling Jolinda disruptive, her teacher is not only personally interpreting Jolinda's behavior but also expressing a hopeless attitude about helping Jolinda change her behavior. *Disruptive* is a general, negative label that makes a value judgment instead of focusing on what Jolinda does to misbehave. Moreover, if Jolinda tunes in to her teacher's attitude, the label "disruptive" could become a self-fulfilling prophecy. The teacher may begin to treat Jolinda as if acting disruptively is expected, and Jolinda may act accordingly.

When we use labels, we run the risk of biasing not only our own relationship with the student but also that of other school personnel, jeopardizing the student's chances for future help and school success:

When Janna walks into Mr. Fox's homeroom next fall, he may anticipate the worst because she's been portrayed as "scattered." Similarly, if Mrs. Kreuter, the school counselor, receives an evaluation that calls Jason "immature," she won't be able to help either Jason or his teacher change the situation. Mrs. Kreuter needs to know exactly what Jason is doing to give his teacher the impression of immaturity. Only with that information can a specific plan be designed to encourage Jason to eliminate the behavior.

Subjective statements and labels also tend not to account for a student maybe behaving differently for different teachers:

Two teachers may describe Jerrod's behavior as "impossible"; four others may view Jerrod as "well adjusted, inquisitive, and studious." Moreover, behavior one teacher views as "inquisitive"—such as asking a lot of questions and constantly suggesting alternative interpretations—may be seen by another as "impossible."

When describing behavior, we can avoid making subjective statements and assigning labels by using emotionally neutral, objective terms. Consider these restatements of the students' behavior:

- "Jerrod sticks his foot in the aisle and trips other second graders about five times each day."
- "Janna fails to hand in English assignments at least three days each week."
- "Jason rocks back and forth in his chair during science and jingles the keys in his pocket during quizzes and tests."
- "When asked to complete his worksheets, Julian makes comments such as 'You can't make me do this' and 'I'm going to use the computer instead.'"
- "Jolinda talks to other students about seven times during history lectures. When asked to stop, she mutters a response under her breath."

If our words say no more and no less than could be recorded by a video camera, our description is probably accurate.

These statements portray behaviors in impersonal, unemotional terms. Instead of interpreting the behaviors, they focus on what actually happens and when it happens.

Record Frequency of Behavior Besides describing behaviors objectively, the previous statements also include information about *how often* a behavior occurs. When we're having difficulty with a student, we tend to think that a behavior occurs more frequently than it actually does. For example, we may be convinced that Evvie taps her pencil "continuously." If we document the frequency of the behavior over several days, we might be surprised to discover that Evvie taps her pencil an average of only four times, and only during social studies.

Another problem with using terms such as *seldom, usually, often, occasionally, frequently,* and *once in a while* is that they mean different things to different people and thus can be interpreted in various ways. Consider this statement: "Ethan is constantly out of his seat." Does it mean that Ethan does not sit down from 9:00 A.M. to 3:00 P.M.? Or that he pops up and walks around the room ten times every hour? Or that he goes to the drinking fountain five or six times a day?

Only when we view troubling behavior in terms of *what, when,* and *how often* are we able to describe it objectively. Such an impartial viewpoint enables us to recognize that changing our interactions with a student is possible, that we can help a student choose more appropriate behavior.

Double-Check Objectivity Here's an easy way to determine if we're describing behavior objectively: If our words say no more and no less than could be recorded by a video camera or tape recorder, our description is probably accurate. Consider Claudia and Clinton:

Claudia stares out the window during math class. A video camera could capture her face turned toward the window and her eyes gazing outside, but it couldn't capture her thoughts. If we were to judge that she is "daydreaming," we might be right or wrong. Claudia might be dreaming of a romantic encounter with the cute fellow in the second row, or she might be thinking about a math problem. We simply don't know what's going on inside of Claudia's head. An objective description of her behavior would be, "Claudia stares out the window."

Clinton may disrupt his neighbors, but exactly how? A video camera could record him passing notes, tapping another student's shoulder, and belching loudly. These behaviors as well as when and how often he does them would make up objective descriptions.

School Action Plan Step 2: Identify the Goal of the Misbehavior

Once we've written objective descriptions of the behaviors causing concern, we're ready to add the goal of the misbehavior. We've already explored the clues to identification of attention, power, revenge, and avoidance-of-failure behavior. Appendix A, Identifying the Four Goals of Misbehavior, provides a summary chart of these clues. When faced with a misbehavior, the answers to the questions that follow will also help us correctly identify the goal.

Attention "Do I feel annoyed or irritated? Is my typical reaction to nag, remind, correct, or rescue? When I do respond, does the misbehavior stop—at least temporarily?" If we answer yes to these questions, the misbehavior is probably for *attention*.

Power "Do I feel angry or frustrated? Is my typical reaction to fight back or give in? Does the misbehavior continue until it stops on the student's terms?" If our answer to this set of questions is yes, the misbehavior is probably for *power*.

Revenge "Do I feel hurt, disappointed, even a sense of dislike for the student? Is my typical reaction to strike back or withdraw? Does the misbehavior intensify before it stops?" If so, we are most likely encountering a bid for *revenge*.

Avoidance-of-Failure "Do I feel professional concern and frustration? Is my typical reaction to give up or make a referral? Does the student continue consistently to avoid the task despite my efforts to help?" When answered yes, this set of questions leads us to identify *avoidance-of-failure* as the goal.

Sometimes the clues are not crystal clear and might seem to overlap. In that case, we can use our intuition and go with the strongest set of clues. If we misidentify the goal, nothing drastic happens. For example, if we incorrectly identify a bid for power as attention seeking and use an intervention strategy that is designed for attention, the student will probably continue to misbehave until we realize what is happening and switch to a graceful exit technique. On the other hand, if we use one of the power interventions when the goal is attention, we'll have worked a little harder than necessary, because most power interventions consume more time and energy than those for attention.

Since clues are not hard facts, we can expect occasional misidentifications. I've been identifying goals of misbehavior for over twenty years and I still have momentary nonsuccesses.

To be effective, the intervention strategy needs to fit the misbehavior.

School Action Plan Step 3: Choose Intervention Techniques for the Moment of Misbehavior

Steps 1 and 2 provide us with the necessary diagnostic information for completing this corrective step of the School Action Plan. In Step 3 we choose one or more of the intervention strategies we learned in Chapters 5, 8, 9, and 12.

Choose first the techniques that make the most sense to you, that fit your teaching style and personality, that are relatively easy to apply, and that are particularly appropriate to your students. Then try other techniques as needed. Most of the techniques are adaptable for use with students of any age, from kindergarten through high school.

School Action Plan Step 4: Select Encouragement Techniques to Build Self-Esteem

If we were to conclude the School Action Plan at Step 3, we could anticipate that the student would misbehave again—today, tomorrow, or the next day. Intervention is a stopgap measure. It ends misbehavior in progress but doesn't necessarily prevent future misbehavior. For this to happen, our interventions must be accompanied by encouragement techniques that strengthen the student's motivation to cooperate and learn.

At Step 4, then, we plot encouragement techniques to help the student feel capable, connected, and contributing.

School Action Plan Step 5: Involve Students, Parents, and Others as Partners

This step reminds us that Cooperative Discipline is just that—a cooperative process that calls for collaboration from the entire school community.

Involving Students We've discussed many ways to make students our partners in the discipline process. When we involve students, we do more than find solutions to today's problem behavior: We teach them information and skills that are transferable to all areas of their lives, now and in the future. In Chapter 19 we will summarize these ideas and explore some additional strategies for guiding students to cooperate.

Involving Parents Seeking the input of parents is equally important. When parents are willing to meet with us in person, the development of a School Action Plan can be a joint effort. Parents can be very insightful as to which intervention strategies and encouragement techniques are most likely to be effective with their children. And once the School Action Plan is completed, we can suggest to parents activities that will support and complement our efforts in the classroom. When parents and teachers use the action plan to work together as partners in the discipline process, young people are greatly influenced to make more responsible choices.[1]

To parents who choose not to meet with us in person, we can mail a copy of the completed School Action Plan so that they are aware of the problems we're experiencing with their son or daughter and how we plan to address them. The plan becomes concrete evidence of our concern and willingness to help their child improve. Because encouragement strategies are included in the plan, this type of discipline notice sent home clearly indicates to parents that we're adopting a *positive*, nonpunishing approach to helping their child. As a result, the next time we request parents' presence at a conference, they just might be more willing to come.

Involving Others The Cooperative Discipline process shows us how fellow teachers, administrators, and school resource personnel can help us help our students. Building the involvement of associates into the action plan serves to remind us that we have many supportive colleagues right in the building.

We can invite other teachers who deal with a misbehaving student to join us in the process of creating a School Action Plan. The cooperative brainstorming that occurs as we complete Steps 1-4 can provide new insight into what's happening in the classroom. This is especially true if the student exhibits Jekyll-and-Hyde behavior, acting appropriately in one teacher's classroom and inappropriately in another's.

The Action Plan Process provides new ideas, mutual support, and a renewed perspective.

There are times when colleagues or other school personnel can help us discipline effectively.

If Mr. Garcia considers Jesse "well adjusted and studious" and Ms. Herrold finds him "disruptive and lazy," a plan for Jesse would be incomplete without the input of *both* Mr. Garcia and Ms. Herrold.

Counselors, psychologists, social workers, and administrators are others we can ask to help us develop a School Action Plan. Since they are not directly involved in any of the classroom interactions that are causing problems, they can provide neutral advice concerning intervention and encouragement techniques.

If more than one teacher is having difficulties with the same student, developing a compatible School Action Plan for each classroom is desirable, as is a similar plan for other school areas such as the library, lunchroom, or study hall. Collaborating in this way can result in a schoolwide action plan that helps everyone be consistent in holding the student accountable for poor behavior choices and in using the Three Cs to encourage more responsible behavior.

Using the School Action Plan as a Monitor of Progress

A School Action Plan should be a living document subject to change. We can review it periodically, noting how the selected interventions and encouragement techniques affect our interactions with the student. We can delete obviously unsuccessful techniques and add new ones.

We need to be tenacious, however, and remember that change takes time. When we change our reactions to students' misbehavior, they sometimes intensify the misbehavior as a means to test our resolve. Our patience *will* pay off. When students see that we're standing firm, unwilling to be manipulated, and continuing to encourage them despite their testing, they begin to make some permanent changes in their behavior choices.

Note

1. A booklet entitled "Bringing Home Cooperative Discipline" (Circle Pines, MN: American Guidance Service, 1994) lists a number of strategies that parents can implement to support the School Action Plan. Many teachers find giving parents a copy at conferences helpful. For information, check with your curriculum specialist or contact American Guidance Service (AGS) at 1-800-328-2560.

CHAPTER 19
Involving Students as Partners

Many ideas for involving students as partners have been presented throughout this book. This chapter will summarize them and explore additional strategies.

Teach Students the Cooperative Discipline Concepts

Before students can actively become partners in the discipline process, they need to know the basic concepts of Cooperative Discipline. Specifically, students need to understand:

- Behavior is based on choice.
- Everyone needs to belong.
- The four goals of misbehavior are attention, power, revenge, and avoidance-of-failure.
- The Three Cs of encouragement are to feel capable, connected, and contributing.
- The code of conduct ensures a safe and orderly classroom for all.

Useful Teaching Resources

While providing you with specific instructions and lesson plans on how to teach these concepts to students is beyond the scope of this book, I can point you toward some useful resources:

Experiential Activities Detailed instructions for a number of experiential activities related to Cooperative Discipline topics are included in the leader's guide for the *Responsible Kids* videos and in the *Cooperative Discipline Implementation Guide*. Many of these activities are as appropriate for secondary students as they are for adults.

In Chapter 12, we briefly discussed Gardner's seven intelligences and identified specific strategies for teaching to each level. Any of these strategies can be used to teach students about Cooperative Discipline.

Involve Students in Selecting Interventions for Misbehavior

The Cooperative Discipline approach gives us two vehicles specifically geared to involving students in solving the problems they create. When used in a conference format, often with the parent, administrator, or counselor in attendance, the questions embedded in these processes lead students to select and to commit themselves to specific behaviors that will eliminate the current problem.

The Six D Conflict Resolution Process We've already seen how we can involve students in this conflict resolution process. Following this process does more than help resolve the issue at hand. It also shows students a model for solving problems in all areas of their lives, including conflicts with classmates.

The Student Action Plan Process The Student Action Plan gives us an additional vehicle for helping students take responsibility for choosing positive behavior. Its purpose is to require students who repeatedly misbehave to reflect on their misbehavior so they can help determine how to avoid letting history repeat itself. Students who are capable of completing the Student Action Plan on their own should do so. Primary students and others lacking the requisite reading and writing skills to complete the plan independently will need our help. Some teachers make a tape-recorded version of the Student Action Plan with a blank space of time left after each question for students to speak and record their responses. Others use a much simplified version of the Student Action Plan, such as this plan used by Dry Creek Elementary School in Rio Linda, California:

Date

I, _____, agree to contribute to the positive, safe, secure environment at Dry Creek School by: _____
_____

If I honor this agreement, I will feel good about my contributions. I will feel capable and connected to all of the people at the school.

If I do not honor this agreement, I will meet with _____ and consequences will result.

Signatures:

Many students take the responsibility of contributing to the classroom very seriously.

As you look at the plan, you'll notice that students having an understanding of the basic Cooperative Discipline concepts is essential for them to answer the questions. Notice, too, that the questions are a modification of the School Action Plan format. Feel free to adapt this generic form and change the wording to reflect the sophistication of your students.

The Student Action Plan can be used in a number of ways.

Teacher-student conference. Teachers can use the plan's questions as the framework for an individual conference. Students can write responses beforehand or answer the questions orally during the conference.

Reentry after time-out. When a student has been sent to time-out, placed in in-school suspension, or referred to a principal, counselor, or dean, the Student Action Plan can be used as a reentry procedure. When we've talked with the student and are satisfied with the student's responses to the questions—especially with the commitment to different behavior in the future—we can invite the student to rejoin the class. It's interesting to note that while most schools have detailed referral procedures, few have a specific process for helping students rejoin the class in a positive manner, prepared to make more responsible choices in the future.

Parent conference. In the next chapter we'll see how the Student Action Plan can be used during parent-teacher and parent-teacher-student discipline conferences. The responses students make to the questions on the plan provide useful data that help in the development of effective School and Home Action Plans.

Involve Students in Creating a Three C Classroom

Once students are familiar with what we mean by *capable, connected,* and *contributing*, they can help publicize the Three Cs so that encouraging behavior becomes the classroom norm.

Student-Created Posters Posters illustrating the Three Cs in action in the classroom can adorn the walls, along with short descriptions of specific Three C behavior students have observed in the classroom.

Three C Wall Charts On each of three large sheets of newsprint, we can write one of these sentence starters:

- *Capable* looks like . . .
- *Connecting* looks like . . .
- *Contributing* looks like . . .

Then we can laminate and post the charts on the walls of the classroom. Students can complete the sentences with descriptions of matching appropriate behaviors. Since they're laminated, the charts can be wiped clean and used again and again.

Banners Banners make an excellent team project for students of all ages. Students will enjoy developing Three C slogans that can be put on banners and hung around the room. Some examples of slogans include:

- I can do it.
- I contribute.
- We're a Three C Classroom!
- High Self-Esteem Zone
- "C" Your Way to Self-Esteem!

Encourage creativity for both the slogans and the decorating of the banners. You and your students might enjoy creating the banners with a computer software program, if your school has one available.

Creative Writing Students can write stories with Three C themes or create skits that depict Three C behaviors. Sharing these with other classes provides reinforcement for the students involved and helps other students learn the concepts.

Three C Committee The group of students who make up this committee have the responsibility of using their creativity to find ways to help all of their classmates fulfill the need to belong. Membership on the committee needs to be rotated so that all students participate and share the responsibility.

A+ Relationships Many of the same strategies we use to connect with students can be shared with the students so that they learn ways to connect with each other.

The responsibility to create a safe and orderly environment belongs to the entire school community.

Involve Students in Creating a Safe and Orderly Environment

Our students want a safe and orderly classroom as much as we do.

The Code of Conduct In Chapter 16 we looked at the process of creating a code of conduct. This process involves students in setting limits for their behavior and in learning how to evaluate their behavior on a moment-to-moment basis.

The Crime Watch Patrol Because violence in schools is increasing, a crime watch patrol (as outlined in Chapter 15) makes good sense. However, we need to make *all* students aware of the problems of illegal behavior in schools and encourage everyone to report any suspicious behavior immediately. The responsibility to create a safe and orderly environment belongs to the entire school community.

Involve Students in the Decision-Making Process

To influence students to choose responsible behavior, we need to adopt a hands-joined management style in which students are treated respectfully as important decision makers who have the right to choose and participate in the design of their education. The most effective vehicle for involving students in the decision-making process is the class meeting.

The Class Meeting The class meeting is a form of the town hall meeting from America's earliest days. Everyone in the meeting is expected to participate, contribute, and accept responsibility for themselves and for the welfare of the class. Secondary school teachers often refer to class meetings as "group meetings" or "total class discussions." Class meetings follow parliamentary procedure and are a microcosm of democracy in action.

We can think of class meetings as the maintenance plan for continued success of in the classroom.

I like to think of class meetings as the maintenance plan for the continued success of the Cooperative Discipline process in the classroom. During these meetings, everyone shares responsibility for "plugging leaks" and "fixing" anything that isn't working quite right. At the same time, general improvements and innovations are added to the original structure when changes are needed.

When class meetings focus on specific Cooperative Discipline issues, discussions can revolve around topics such as:

- dealing with attention-seeking, power, revenge, or avoidance-of-failure behaviors observed in class
- helping all students feel capable, connected, and contributing
- reviewing or revising the classroom code of conduct

We can also use class meetings to make announcements, discuss student gripes, plan class activities and projects, organize field trips, assign classroom jobs and responsibilities, and make academic choices.

While class meetings are appropriate to all grade levels K-12, the structure, content, frequency, and length of the meeting varies depending upon the age and maturity of the students. Ground rules need to be established in advance. In secondary classrooms, a student chairperson typically conducts the meeting and a designated note-taker records all decisions.

CHAPTER 20
Involving Parents as Partners

Parents play a vital role in the Cooperative Discipline process. We need them to help boost their child's self-esteem. We need them to help teach their child that misbehaving for attention, power, or revenge, or to avoid failure doesn't pay off. When parents and teachers—the most significant adults in a young person's life—establish common goals and use compatible strategies, the Cooperative Discipline process has the greatest chance for success.

With Cooperative Discipline we can set up a realistic parent-teacher partnership. Parents cannot directly alleviate discipline problems that occur in school any more than teachers can control discipline matters at home. We therefore ask parents to work on discipline problems at home, while we work on those that occur during the school day. Together, we cooperate to set up action plans appropriate for both home and school. Young people, of course, benefit from experiencing the same approach in both places.

Discipline problems in school frequently mirror discipline problems in the home, since the same forces that work against effective discipline procedures often exist in both places. To help parents recognize these shared problems and to convince them to become our partners in the discipline process, we need to offer them information about effective intervention and encouragement strategies to use at home.

This is not really a new role for us. In most parent-teacher conferences, we probably already ask parents to do certain things at home to help their children behave better in school. In using the Cooperative Discipline approach, we simply become more efficient and effective providers of parent education. We have at our fingertips a variety of strategies that parents can use to mirror and reinforce what we're doing in the classroom.

Convincing parents to become our partners in the discipline process is usually not a hard sell. In many communities, parents view school personnel as the most approachable, and perhaps the only, source of guidance for dealing with misbehavior.

It's no secret that young people from homes with effective intervention and encouragement strategies cause less difficulty in school than those from homes with lax or ineffective discipline. So any work we do to educate parents benefits us directly as well as our students. We may even discover that as parent effectiveness improves, student achievement scores go up. A team of researchers headed by Sanford M. Dornbusch at Stanford University Center for the Study of Families, Children, and Youth found that a link exists between parenting styles and children's academic performance.[1] The cooperative

Parents can reinforce what we're doing in the classroom.

(hands-joined) style correlates with the highest grades, whereas both autocratic (hands-on) and permissive (hands-off) parenting styles are associated with lower grades.

Educating parents about effective discipline is not as difficult a job as we might think, particularly since the theoretical framework of Cooperative Discipline is translated into the School Action Plan. We've already seen how the School Action Plan provides a format for discussion, enabling us to share information and concerns with parents.

Informing Parents About Cooperative Discipline

The best time to inform parents about the Cooperative Discipline approach is *before* any problems occur. In this way, we greatly increase the chances of a supportive response rather than a defensive reaction from parents if we do experience difficulties with their child. When parents understand what the Cooperative Discipline process involves—encouragement strategies as well as interventions—they usually become willing partners, backing our efforts in the classroom and receptive to our suggestions about what reinforcement steps may be taken at home.

Newsletter Column If you regularly distribute a parent newsletter or information sheet, include a column entitled "The Discipline Corner." Use it to highlight specific interventions and encouragement strategies within the Cooperative Discipline process. In this way, parents are kept informed about efforts being made to improve student behavior and gain some ideas they can use at home as well.

Parent Resource Library Some teachers like to keep a collection of resource books on hand for lending to parents. If your school library doesn't have a parent resource library, consider helping establish one, developing one of your own, or collaborating with other teachers to gather a variety of books on discipline and self-esteem.[2]

Parent Drop-In Center You might wish to spearhead taking the resource library one step further, setting aside a special room at school where parents can drop in for a cup of coffee and browse through the information. At specific times, a teacher, counselor, school psychologist, social worker, or administrator could be on hand to discuss parental concerns about discipline at home or school.

Parent Group Presentations You may wish to talk to your principal or site council about devoting a portion of PTA-PTO meetings to helping parents learn the Cooperative Discipline philosophy and strategies.

The best time to inform parents about the Cooperative Discipline approach is before any problems occur

Guidelines for Establishing an Atmosphere of Mutual Support

It's up to us to ensure that phone calls and conferences inspire parental cooperation instead of defensive hostility. To encourage positive responses, we can keep some guidelines in mind.

Use Objective Terms To win cooperation, talking about behavior in objective, nonjudgmental terms is critical. For a quick refresher, review the section "Avoid Subjective Terms" in Chapter 18. This guideline is every bit as true when describing students' behavior to parents—in fact, maybe more so. A parent who hears, "Winona is almost constantly disruptive," is more likely to react defensively than if told, "Winona calls out answers without raising her hand about five times a day."

To win parental cooperation, it's critical that we talk about behavior in nonjudgmental terms.

Limit the Number of Complaints Mentioning every transgression that a student has ever committed will stagger even the most cooperative of parents. If we give just a few choice examples of the misbehavior causing the most concern, parents can grasp what's going on without being deluged by bad news.

Avoid Predicting Future Failures "Mr. Palermo, if your daughter doesn't stop this behavior soon, she'll never get a high school diploma." Just hearing how their child is behaving today is usually enough for parents to bear without the added worry about what the child might or might not be doing a year from now.

Anticipate Success We want to avoid giving parents the impression that we consider their child incorrigible. If we throw up our hands and sigh, "I don't know what to do with your son," parents will lose confidence in us, themselves, and their child. A better approach is to show parents that we've thought a great deal about their child by presenting a specific plan—the School Action Plan. If we also mention some positive behaviors and predict success, we are usually rewarded with favorable parental responses.

Don't Take Defensiveness Personally A defensive response to upsetting news is natural. When children cause problems in school, parents often react defensively to cover up how they actually feel— guilty, powerless, fearful, and overwhelmed. Let's take a closer look at each of these feelings, for when we understand how parents feel, we're better able to respond empathically.

Guilty. Since many parents believe that behavior is *caused* rather than *chosen*, they blame themselves for not being good enough parents.

Powerless. Parents think they are supposed to know how to make their children behave, both at home and at school. When parents realize that their discipline efforts aren't working, they wind up feeling powerless.

Fearful. When teachers describe today's problems, many parents are gnawed by fears about the future. "If my six year old is disturbing others and not paying attention in first grade, what will happen when he gets to middle school?" "If my fifteen year old is cutting classes today, will she drop out and end up on the street next year?"

Overwhelmed. Balancing home and work isn't easy, especially for a single parent. Many parents work outside the home during the day and attempt to fulfill all their parenting and housekeeping duties during evenings and weekends. When we tell already overwhelmed parents about their child's classroom problems, we could be adding the straw that breaks the camel's back.

Ask for the Possible

Sometimes parents get impossible requests from teachers. "Mrs. MacDougall, please talk to Scottie and make sure he doesn't come to class late any more." "Mr. Capistrant, please impress upon Laurel that her attitude and work habits must improve if she's to pass algebra this year." When parents receive requests like these, they may feel justifiably upset, for they may not know how to accomplish such tasks. The consequences for inappropriate behavior in school need to be established and enforced by the teacher, not the parents. Long-distance discipline doesn't work. Any requests made of parents are best described in the form of specific actions that can be taken at home.

> *At times, we all find balancing home and work overwhelming.*

Notifying Parents When Behavior Problems Occur

When we're having sufficient difficulty with a student to warrant developing a School Action Plan, we need to call parents to let them know that a problem exists. This personal contact can help us form a congenial relationship with the parents, especially when we use the "sandwich technique" of beginning with a positive statement about the child, stating the problem, and ending with another positive statement.

If we've already informed parents about our Cooperative Discipline approach, they'll know that a School Action Plan is formulated when a student repeatedly misbehaves. During a phone call, we can offer two options: Either we'll develop an action plan ourselves and send home a completed copy, or we'll set up a conference with the parents and develop the plan together. A second phone call is necessary to parents who choose not to attend a conference. At this point, we can answer parents' questions about the plan and let them know that we are willing to help them devise strategies for supporting the School Action Plan and also to formulate a similar Home Action Plan. In all cases we proceed to develop a School Action Plan and continuously involve parents in the process by making frequent calls home or sending notes to celebrate successes as they occur.

What if parents reject any involvement in the School Action Plan and refuse a Home Action Plan? Although our job will be more difficult without parental partnership, we still can achieve some results in our classrooms. Young people don't necessarily expect all adults to react the same when they misbehave. They know that what works with Mom won't always work with Dad, and what works with Dad won't always work with the teacher. If we use sound classroom discipline procedures and follow through carefully on interventions and encouragement strategies, we can at least make a difference when the student is with us. In some cases, we'll have to settle for that.

Structuring the Parent-Teacher Conference

Talking with parents about their child's misbehavior and eliciting their support can be tricky. As we've seen, some parents might become defensive or blame the teacher for their child's disruptive behavior. A number of Cooperative Discipline strategies and resources can be combined to produce successful parent-teacher conferences.

Begin With the A+ Strategies

The Five A's for helping students connect can also be used with parents. These strategies ensure a good start to the conference.

Acceptance We relate to parents without prejudice or stereotypes based on race, gender, background, or family structure.

Attention We give attention undividedly. How we sit, listen, and respond makes or breaks the positive connection we seek.

Appreciation We use positive appreciation statements for parents' attendance and support, as well as for positive behaviors exhibited by their child.

Affirmation We validate the child's strengths including social, emotional, and academic traits, behaviors, and achievements.

Affection We let parents know that we care for their child.

Discuss the Student Action Plan

If the student in question has completed the Student Action Plan form, use this to start the discussion of the misbehavior. This Student Action Plan lets the parent understand the misbehavior from the child's point of view, along with the child's plan for choosing more responsible behavior in the future.

Develop the School Action Plan

Prior to the conference we can complete Steps 1 and 2 of the School Action Plan and tentatively identify strategies for Steps 3 and 4. It's important to ask for parental input at Steps 3 and 4 before the plan is finalized. A parent won't feel like a true partner if we present a fait accompli, nor would we be able to take advantage of the helpful insights the parent has about what works with his or her child. As we're developing the School Action Plan together, the parent gains an understanding of the Cooperative Discipline theory and learns some strategies to use at home to support our efforts. Appendixes A-D in this book are useful resources to share with the parent during this process.

Once the School Action Plan is completed, we can invite parents to continue to participate in the Cooperative Discipline process. They may choose to become silent partners who receive periodic reports about their child's behavioral progress, or they may want to become active partners, eager to devise a Home Action Plan that will reinforce the School Action Plan and alleviate behavior problems at home.

Create a Home Action Plan

Ask parents to describe the misbehavior as objectively as possible.

The question to ask parents is, "At home, do you see behavior similar to what I see in school?" The answer could be yes or no. If no similar discipline problems are to be worked on at home, then we can concentrate on helping parents plan some encouragement strategies they can use to boost their child's self-esteem. The higher the child's self-esteem, the easier to correct misbehavior in the classroom.

More likely than not, however, parents will admit that they are bothered at home by behaviors similar to those we've observed in the classroom. When this is the case, we can offer to assist parents in developing a Home Action Plan that follows the first four steps of the School Action Plan.

Step 1: Pinpoint and Describe Behavior Ask the parents to describe the misbehavior as objectively as possible. Their objective descriptions are written under Step 1 of the plan.

Step 2: Identify the Goal Use Appendix A, Identifying the Four Goals of Misbehavior, and Appendix B, Understanding the Goals of Misbehavior, to help parents determine the goal of the misbehavior occurring at home. This goal is written under Step 2 of the plan.

If parents identify more than one goal of misbehavior, encourage them to work first on attention-seeking or avoidance-of-failure behaviors since these tend to be easier to deal with than power or revenge behaviors. Once parents have experienced some success, they'll feel encouraged to tackle the more difficult behaviors.

Step 3: Choose Intervention Techniques

Use Appendix C, Summary Chart of Interventions, to help parents explore options for handling misbehaviors at home. While we can recommend which interventions to use, parents should make the final choice. Their selected interventions are written under Step 3 of the plan.

Assisting parents in choosing interventions for power or revenge behaviors is probably the most difficult step in helping devise a Home Action Plan. This is because the home application of many of the strategies is somewhat different from our school application. For example, parents can make a graceful exit by simply walking out of a room, leaving the child who is spouting I-hate-you statements alone. As teachers, we don't have this option. Likewise, some of the options we may have, such as sending a child to another classroom, are unavailable to parents.

A book you'll probably find helpful when completing Step 3 of the Home Action Plan is *Coping With Kids*.[3] This book identifies specific interventions for use in over 100 different situations.

Step 4: Select Encouragement Techniques

Talk about various encouragement techniques with parents, but allow them to decide which to include under Step 4 of the plan. Use the summary chart of encouragement techniques in Appendix D—The Building Blocks of Self-Esteem—to identify which techniques to use.

If time doesn't permit, or if we don't feel confident assisting parents with home problems, we can ask a counselor, psychologist, or trained parent volunteer to offer this assistance.

Schedule a Follow-Up Conversation

At the end of the conference, set a date for a follow-up in about two weeks. This can be either a phone conversation or a meeting during which we can check to see how well the action plans are working. Further phone conversations or meetings on a regular basis will allow us to monitor progress and help modify either the School or the Home Action Plan as needed.

If the student's behavior begins to improve at home, school, or both places, the same intervention and encouragement strategies can be retained. If the misbehavior has not decreased, changes need to be made in Steps 3 and 4 of the action plan. Often it's helpful for an administrator, a counselor, or a colleague to offer advice when making these changes.

Structuring the Parent-Teacher-Student Discipline Conference

If a child is old enough to misbehave in school, the child can help create a plan to end the problem.

When we invite students to join us and their parents in a discipline conference, we are putting some of the responsibility for solving behavior problems where it belongs—on the students. Since the purpose of the Action Plan Process is intended to help students choose more appropriate behavior, their insight about the problem and possible solutions can be invaluable. Moreover, when students realize that their parents and teachers are jointly determined to end the misbehavior, most usually begin to understand that it's time to make a change. My motto: If a child is old enough to misbehave in school, the child is old enough to be involved in creating a plan to end the problem.

Meet First With the Parent Before involving the student in the conference, we first may want to meet privately with the parents to solidify the relationship using the A+ strategies and to exchange confidential information. When the student joins us, we can use the Student Action Plan as a framework for discussion. If the form was completed before the conference, the discussion can focus on the student's responses. If not, it can be completed at this time. We can ask for clarification as needed and, with the parents, work and rework each step of the Student Action Plan until everyone feels a practical plan has been created.

Focus on the Future Caution must be taken to keep the main focus of the discussion on the future. Since the past can't be changed, searching for the "causes" of the misbehavior or listening to student excuses isn't helpful. The focus needs to be on the future, on preventing the misbehavior from reoccurring. We can cut off any digressions by insisting, "Let's talk only about what we can do so that the behavior doesn't happen again."

Some teachers excuse the student after the Student Action Plan has been discussed and continue to develop the School and Home Action Plans alone with parents. Others, especially secondary teachers, prefer to have the student be part of the entire conference. Either way works. It's a matter of personal preference and comfort level.

Getting School Support for Parents as Partners

Classroom teachers can't always do it alone. We may need help from others in the school community to support our efforts to enlist parents as partners in the discipline process.

School Specialists Because of their specialized training, school counselors, psychologists, and social workers can be most helpful in explaining to parents how to apply the Cooperative Discipline procedures at home and in devising intervention and encouragement strategies. As neutral observers not directly involved in any of the interactions that are causing problems, they can provide an invaluable perspective on the misbehavior. When invited to participate in a conference with teacher, parent, and student, these support personnel can use their mediation skills to deal with any misunderstanding or disagreement that may arise among the participants. Since they're trained in understanding emotions, they can help a participant express and cope with strong feelings.

Administrators If we're dealing with a student who has sought revenge by damaging school property or the possessions of others or whose behavior threatens others' safety, we may want to invite a school administrator to join a conference. The administrator's role would be similar to that of a counselor or psychologist—an impartial participant. Moreover, the presence of an administrator, as a representative of the ultimate authority in the school, often impresses the seriousness of the matter at hand on the student better than any verbal admonitions.

When we invite the participation of parents, students, specialists, or administrators in the discipline process, we're on our way to establishing cooperative relationships that can make a difference in our students' behavior in and beyond the classroom, today and tomorrow.

The parent-teacher-student conference puts an end to students playing school against home.

Notes

1. *Parenting*, December 1987, 16.
2. If your school has a copy of the *Cooperative Discipline Implementation Guide* (Circle Pines, MN: American Guidance Service, 1995), you can ask to see the lists of parent resource materials it includes. You may also want to purchase or have your school purchase copies of *Bringing Home Cooperative Discipline* (Circle Pines, MN: American Guidance Service, 1994), an appealing, illustrated eight-page booklet that tells parents about the Cooperative Discipline approach in very brief, simple terms; and *Responsible Kids in School and at Home* (Circle Pines, MN: American Guidance Service, 1994), a set of videos appropriate for both teachers and parents.
3. Linda Albert, *Coping With Kids* (Tampa, FL: Alkorn House, 1993).

*P*erhaps the question teachers most often ask me is, "Do you believe today's students are different from the students we used to have—five, ten, fifteen years ago?"

My answer: Yes and no.

The basic psychological needs of students have not changed. All young people still need to belong: to feel capable, connected, and contributing. I believe that one hundred years from now teachers will still have to use encouragement strategies to help students satisfy these basic needs.

Students have always *chosen* their behavior—that hasn't changed during the thirty-plus years I've been involved in education. What has changed, however, are the choices young people are making today. While we once worried about students chewing gum, today we worry about students toting guns.

We can't teach the students we *used to have*. Or those we *wish we had*. We must teach the students *we do have*—all students, including those who bring their "choosing disabilities" into our classroom, disrupt our teaching, and exhibit angry, disturbing, and even potentially violent behavior.

Creating solutions to classroom disruptions and school violence, establishing safe and orderly classrooms, and helping *all* students choose cooperative behavior involves implementing the Cooperative Discipline approach in its entirety: Using the hands-joined management style; consistently applying the intervention and encouragement strategies; establishing a code of conduct and conflict resolution procedures; following the Action Plan Process; involving students, parents, and others. No one piece of the puzzle is as powerful and effective as all the pieces put together.

Perhaps the hardest lesson I've ever learned about life is that change begins with me. If I wait for others to change first, I might wait forever—and become discouraged and disillusioned while I wait. When I gave up wishing my students were different and started to implement the Cooperative Discipline strategies in my classroom, I found that students began to change. The more I changed what I was doing, the more they changed what they were doing. We teachers *do* make a difference. We have tremendous power to influence students' choices.

BIBLIOGRAPHY

Albert, Linda. *An Administrator's Guide to Cooperative Discipline*. Circle Pines, MN: American Guidance Service, 1992.

———. "Bringing Home Cooperative Discipline" (booklet). Circle Pines, MN: American Guidance Service, 1994.

———. *Coping With Kids*. Tampa, FL: Alkorn House, 1993.

———. *Coping With Kids and School*. New York: Ballantine, 1985.

Albert, Linda, and Michael Popkin. *Quality Parenting*. New York: Ballantine, 1989.

Bettner, Betty Lou, and Amy Lew. *Raising Kids Who Can*. New York: HarperCollins, 1992.

Bluestein, Jane. *21st Century Discipline*. Jefferson City, MO: Scholastic, 1990.

Bowman, Robert P., and John N. Chanaca. *Peer Pals: Kids Helping Kids Succeed in School*. Circle Pines, MN: American Guidance Service, 1994.

Brendtro, L. K., M. Brokenleg, and S. Van Bockern. *Reclaiming Youth at Risk*. Bloomington, IN: National Educational Service, 1990.

Brooks, Robert. *The Self-Esteem Teacher*. Circle Pines, MN: American Guidance Service, 1991.

Canfield, Jack, and Mark Victor Hansen. *Chicken Soup for the Soul*. Deerfield Beach, FL: Health Communications, 1993.

Cangelosi, James S. *Cooperation in the Classroom*. 2d ed. Washington, DC: National Education Association, 1990.

Charles, C. M. *Building Classroom Discipline*. 4th ed. New York: Longman, 1992.

Clark, Barbara. *Growing Up Gifted*. 3d ed. New York: Macmillan, 1988.

Connection and Clear Limits, program 1 in *Gangs and Group Violence*. Louisville: AGS Media, 1995.

Cool 2B Safe (video program). St. Paul: Wilder Foundation, 1995.

Curran, Dolores. *Working With Parents: Dolores Curran's Guide to Successful Parent Groups*. Circle Pines, MN: American Guidance Service, 1989.

Dinkmeyer, Don, Gary D. McKay, and Don Dinkmeyer, Jr. *Systematic Training for Effective Teaching (STET)*. Circle Pines, MN: American Guidance Service, 1983.

Dinkmeyer, Don, Gary D. McKay, James S. Dinkmeyer, and Don Dinkmeyer, Jr. *Teaching and Leading Children: Training for Supportive Guidance of Children Under Six*. Circle Pines, MN: American Guidance Service, 1992.

Dreikurs, Rudolf. *Psychology in the Classroom*. New York: Harper and Row, 1957, 1968.

Dreikurs, Rudolf, Bernice Bronia Grunwald, and Floy C. Pepper. *Maintaining Sanity in the Classroom*. 2d ed. New York: HarperCollins, 1990.

Dubelle, Stanley T., Jr., and Carol M. Hoffman. *Misbehavin': Solving the Disciplinary Puzzle for Educators*. Lancaster, PA: Technomic Publishing, 1984.

———. *Misbehavin' II*. Lancaster, PA: Technomic Publishing, 1986.

Frymier, J., and B. Gansneder. "The Phi Delta Kappa Study of Students at Risk," in *Phi Delta Kappan* 71 (no. 2): 142-6.

Gardner, Howard. *Frames of Mind: The Theory of Multiple Intelligences*. New York: Harper and Row, 1983.

Gathercoal, Forrest. *Judicious Discipline*. Ann Arbor, MI: Caddo Gap Press, 1990.

Ginott, Chaim G. *Teacher and Child: A Book for Parents and Teachers*. New York: Basic Books, 1993.

Glasser, William. *Control Theory in the Classroom*. New York: HarperCollins, 1986.

———. *The Quality School*. 2d ed., rev. and expanded. New York: HarperCollins, 1992.

———. *Schools Without Failure*. New York: HarperCollins, 1975.

Glenn, H. Stephen, and Jane Nelsen. *Raising Children for Success*. Fair Oaks, CA: Sunrise Press, 1987.

Gossen, Diane Chelsom. *Restitution*. Chapel Hill, NC: New View Publications, 1992.

Handling Student Conflicts: A Positive Approach. Miami, FL: Grace Contrino Abrams Peace Education Foundation, 1993.

Hartmann, Thomas. *Attention Deficit Disorder: A Different Perception*. Lancaster, PA: Underwood-Miller, 1993.

Henderson, Anne, Carl Marburger, and Theodora Ooms. *Beyond the Bake Sale: An Educator's Guide to Working With Parents*. Columbia, MD: National Committee for Citizens in Education, 1986.

Hendrick, Joanne. *The Whole Child: New Trends in Early Education*. St. Louis: Mosby, 1980.

Kohn, Alfie. *Punished by Rewards*. New York: Houghton Mifflin, 1993.

Kreidler, William J. *Creative Conflict Resolution*. New York: GoodYearBooks, 1983.

LePage, Andy. *Transforming Education*. Oakland, CA: Oakmore House, 1987.

Martin, Robert. *Teaching Through Encouragement*. Englewood Cliffs, NJ: Prentice Hall, 1980.

Molnar, A., and B. Linquist. *Changing Problem Behavior in Schools*. San Francisco: Jossey-Bass, 1990.

Nelsen, Jane. *Positive Discipline*. New York: Ballantine, 1987.

Page, Parker, and Dan Cieloha. *Getting Along: A Program for Developing Skills in Cooperation, Caring for Others, Critical Thinking, and Positive Conflict Resolution*. Circle Pines, MN: American Guidance Service, 1990.

Reasoner, Robert W. *Building Self-Esteem in the Elementary Schools*. 2d ed., rev. Palo Alto, CA: Consulting Psychologists Press, 1992.

Sprick, Randall. *Discipline in the Secondary Classroom*. West Nyack, NY: Center for Applied Research in Education, 1985.

Weiner, Bernard. "Principles for a Theory of Student Motivation and Their Application Within an Attributional Framework," in *Research on Motivation in Education: Student Motivation*. Vol. I, eds. Russell E. Ames and Carole Ames. New York: Academic Press, 1984.

Wilson, John H. *The Invitational Elementary Classroom*. Springfield, IL: Charles C. Thomas, 1986.

Wlodkowski, Raymond J., and Judith H. Jaynes. *Eager to Learn*. San Francisco: Jossey-Bass, 1990.

Wong, Harry K., and Rosemary T. Wong. *The First Days of School*. Sunnyvale, CA: Harry K. Wong Publications, 1991.

Wright, Esther. *Loving Discipline*. San Francisco: Teaching From the Heart, 1994.

Youngs, Bettie B. *Enhancing Self-Esteem for Educators: Your Criteria*. No.1. Torrance, CA: Jalmar Press, 1993.

WHAT'S THE STUDENT'S MESSAGE?	HOW DO I FEEL? (Clue 1)	WHAT DO I USUALLY DO?* (Clue 2)	AS A RESULT, WHAT DOES THE STUDENT DO? (Clue 3)	GOAL
"Look at me!"	Irritated, annoyed	Remind, nag, scold, rescue	Stops temporarily	Attention
"Let's fight."	Angry, frustrated	Fight back, give in	Continues, stops on own terms	Power
"I'll get even!"	Angry, hurt, disappointed, sense of dislike	Retaliate, punish severely, withdraw	Continues and intensifies, stops on own terms	Revenge
"Leave me alone."	Professional concern, frustration	Give up trying, refer student to support services	Continues avoiding tasks	Avoidance-of-Failure

Remember that these typical reactions actually reinforce the misbehavior.

	ATTENTION-SEEKING BEHAVIOR	POWER BEHAVIOR
Active Characteristics	*Active AGMs:* Student does all kinds of behaviors that distract teacher and classmates.	*Temper tantrums and verbal tantrums:* Student is disruptive and confrontive.
Passive Characteristics	*Passive AGMs:* Student exhibits one-pea-at-a-time behavior, operates on slow, slower, slowest speeds.	*Quiet noncompliance:* Student does his or her own thing, yet often is pleasant and even agreeable.
Origins of Behavior	Parents and teachers tend to pay more attention to misbehavior than to appropriate behavior. Young people aren't taught how to ask for attention appropriately. Young people may be deprived of sufficient personal attention.	*Hiding behind a label:* Transforms bid for power into inherent personality trait. Changes in society that stress equality in relationships, rather than dominant-submissive roles. The exaltation of the individual and the emphasis on achieving personal power, as epitomized by the human potential movement.
Students' Legitimate Needs	Positive recognition	Personal autonomy
Silver Lining	Student wants a relationship with the teacher (and classmates).	Student exhibits leadership potential, assertiveness, and independent thinking.
Principles of Prevention	1. Catch student being good by giving lots of attention for appropriate behavior. 2. Teach student to ask directly for attention when needed.	1. Allow voice and choice so student has options and feels heard. 2. Grant legitimate power through hands-joined discipline and decision making. 3. Delegate responsibility so student feels sense of responsible power. 4. Avoid and defuse confrontations.

REVENGE BEHAVIOR	AVOIDANCE-OF-FAILURE BEHAVIOR
Physical and psychological attacks: Student is hurtful to teacher, classmates, or both.	*Frustration tantrum:* Student loses control when pressure to succeed becomes too intense.
Student is sullen and withdrawn, refusing overtures of friendship.	Student procrastinates, fails to complete projects, develops temporary incapacity, or assumes behaviors that resemble a learning disability.
A reflection of the increasing violence in society. Media role models that solve conflicts by force.	Rule of the red pencil. Unreasonable expectations of parents and teachers. Student's belief that only perfection is acceptable; student's star mentality. Emphasis on competition in the classroom.
Safety and security	Success
Student shows a spark of life by trying to protect self from further hurt.	Student may want to succeed if can be assured of not making mistakes and of achieving some status. For some severely discouraged students, there is no silver lining.
1. Build a caring relationship with the student. 2. Teach student how to express hurt and hostility appropriately and invite student to talk to us when she or he is upset.	1. Encourage an "I can," rather than "I can't," belief. 2. Foster friendships to end social isolation.

	GENERAL STRATEGY	TECHNIQUES
Attention-Seeking Behavior	Minimize the attention.	Refuse to respond. Give "The Eye." Stand close by. Use name dropping. Send a general signal. Send a secret signal. Give written notice. Use an I-message.
	Clarify desired behavior.	State "Grandma's Law." Use "target-stop-do."
	Legitimize the behavior.	Create a lesson from the misbehavior. Go the distance. Have the class join in. Use a diminishing quota.
	Do the unexpected.	Turn out the lights. Play a musical sound. Lower your voice. Change your voice. Talk to the wall. Use one-liners. Cease teaching temporarily.
	Distract the student.	Ask a direct question. Ask a favor. Give choices. Change the activity.
	Notice appropriate behavior.	Use proximity praise. Use compliance praise. Make recordings. Give a standing ovation.
	Move the student.	Change the student's seat. Use the thinking chair.

Power and Revenge Behaviors	Make a graceful exit.	Acknowledge students' power.
		Remove the audience.
		Table the matter.
		Schedule a conference.
		Use a fogging technique:
		    Agree with the student.
		    Change the subject.
		State both viewpoints.
		Refuse responsibility.
		Dodge irrelevant issues.
		Deliver a closing statement.
		Call the student's bluff.
		Take teacher time-out.

GENERAL STRATEGY	TECHNIQUES
Use time-out.	Use the language of choice. Call the who squad. Require a reentry plan.
Set consequences. Loss or delay of privileges:	Loss or delay of activity. Loss or delay of using objects. Loss or delay of access to school areas.
Loss of freedom of interaction:	Denied interactions with other students. Required interactions with school personnel. Required interactions with parents. Required interactions with police.
Restitution:	Return, repair, or replacement of objects. Repayment of time. Compensation to classmates and teachers. School service.
Reteach appropriate behavior:	Extended practice. Written reports.
Conduct a teacher-student conference.	

	GENERAL STRATEGY	TECHNIQUES
Avoidance-of-Failure Behavior[*]	Modify instructional methods.	Use concrete learning materials. Use computer-based instruction. Teach one step at a time. Teach to the seven intelligences.
	Encourage positive self-talk.	Post positive classroom signs. Require two "put-ups" for every put-down. Encourage positive self-talk before tasks.
	Reframe the "I can't" refrain.	State your belief in students' abilities. Stage an "I can't" funeral.
	Teach procedures for becoming "unstuck."	Brainstorm ask-for-help gambits. Use sequence charts.
	Provide tutoring	

The "capable" strategies in Appendix D are additional strategies that can be used as intervention techniques for avoidance-of-failure behaviors.

HELPING STUDENTS FEEL CAPABLE

Make mistakes okay.
Talk about mistakes.
Equate mistakes with effort.
Minimize mistakes' effect.

Build confidence.
Focus on improvement.
Notice contributions.
Build on strengths.
Show faith in students.
Acknowledge a task's
    difficulty.
Set time limits on tasks.

Focus on past successes.
Analyze past success.
Repeat past success.

Make learning tangible.
"I-Can" cans.
Accomplishment albums
    and portfolios.
Checklists of skills.
Flowchart of concepts.
Talks about yesterday,
    today, and tomorrow.

Recognize achievement.
Applause.
Clapping and standing
    ovations.
Stars and stickers.
Awards and assemblies.
Exhibits.
Positive time-out.
Self-approval.

HELPING STUDENTS CONNECT

Give students the Five A's as much and as often as possible:

Acceptance.
Accept students' cultural differences.
Accept students with disabilities.
Accept students' personal style.
Accept the doer, not the deed.

Attention.
Greet students.
Listen to students:
Teach students to ask for attention.
Spend time chatting.
Ask students about their life outside school.
Mention what you've talked about before.
Eat with students.
Invite students to eat in your room.
Attend school events.
Get involved in a project with students.
Schedule individual conferences.
Join students on the playground.
Chaperon school events.
Recognize birthdays.
Make baby-picture bulletin boards.
Send cards, messages, homework
    to absent students.
Show interest in students' work or hobbies.

Appreciation.
Appreciate the deed, not the doer.
Use three-part appreciation statements.
Give written words of appreciation.
Teach students to ask for appreciation.

Affirmation.
Be specific: Affirm the doer, not the deed.
Be enthusiastic.
Acknowledge positive traits verbally
    or in writing.
Be a talent scout.

Affection.
Give affection with no strings attached.
Show affection when things go badly.
Show kindness, and it will multiply and be
    returned: Affection breeds affection.
Show friendship.
Use affectionate touch when appropriate.

HELPING STUDENTS CONTRIBUTE

Encourage students' contributions to the class.
Involve students in building
    the learning environment.
Invite students' help with
    daily tasks.
Request students' curriculum
    choices.
Designate class liaisons.
Appoint reporters.
Delegate responsibility for
    specific functions.

Encourage students' contributions to the school.
Appoint area monitors.
Create a Three C committee.
Schedule work service
    periods.
Establish a crime watch
    patrol.

Encourage students' contributions to the community.
Adopt a health care center.
Adopt a zoo animal.
Contribute to community
    drives.
Promote volunteerism.
Acknowledge random acts of
    kindness.

Encourage students to work to protect the environment.
Join and support a cause.
Take part in school and
    community recycling,
    clean-up, and antilitter
    campaigns.

Encourage students to help other students.
Circle of friends.
Peer tutoring.
Peer counseling.
Peer mediation.
Peer recognition.

Step 1. Define the problem objectively. _____

_____

Step 2. Describe the feelings of student and teacher.
Student feelings: _____
Teacher feelings: _____

Step 3. Declare the needs of student and teacher.
Student needs: _____
Teacher needs: _____

Step 4. Discuss and evaluate potential solutions.
Solution 1: _____

Advantages	Disadvantages
1.	1.
2.	2.
3.	3.

Solution 2: _____

Advantages	Disadvantages
1.	1.
2.	2.
3.	3.

Solution 3: _____

Advantages	Disadvantages
1.	1.
2.	2.
3.	3.

Step 5. Decide on a plan. _____

_____

Date effectiveness to be evaluated: _____

Step 6. Determine effectiveness. Plan working?_____ Plan not working? _____
Modifications needed: _____

_____

Student Signature _____
Teacher Signature _____
Today's Date _____ Evaluate and follow up on (date) _____

Student _____ Teacher _____ Date _____

Step 1: Pinpoint and describe the student's behavior.

Behavior   Occurred how often?

1. _____   _____

2. _____   _____

3. _____   _____

Step 2: Identify the goal for each behavior you have listed. Use the clues listed. *Hint: Circle or highlight the clues for each behavior in a different color.*

Emotional Pressure Gauge	How Did I Feel?	What Did I Do?	How Did the Student Respond?	Goal
	Irritated, annoyed	Reminded, nagged, scolded	Stopped temporarily	Attention
	Angry, frustrated	Fought back, gave in	Continued, stopped on own terms	Power
	Angry, hurt, disappointed sense of dislike	Retaliated, punished severely, withdrew	Continued, intensified, stopped on own terms	Revenge
	Professional concern, frustration	Gave up trying, referred for support services	Continued avoiding tasks	Avoidance-of-failure

Step 3: Choose interventions to stop the misbehavior. *Use Appendix C. First decide which strategies seem most applicable, then select the specific techniques you will use to implement each strategy. When using consequences, be specific about what, where, and when the consequences will occur.*

Goal   **Strategies**

Attention   Minimize the attention, clarify desired behavior, legitimize the behavior, do the unexpected, distract the student, notice appropriate behavior, move the student.

Techniques   _____

                   _____

                   _____

Power or   Make a graceful exit, use time-out, set consequences, schedule a conference.
Revenge

Techniques   _____

                   _____

                   _____

| Avoidance-of-Failure | Modify instructional methods, provide tutoring, encourage positive self-talk, reframe the "I can't" refrain, teach ways to get "unstuck," make mistakes okay, build confidence, focus on past successes, make learning tangible, recognize achievement. |

Techniques _____

_____

_____

Step 4: Select encouragement strategies to satisfy the need to belong and to build self-esteem.

C
Capable

Strategies
Make mistakes okay, build confidence, focus on past successes, make learning tangible, recognize achievement.

Techniques _____

_____

_____

Connect

Acceptance, attention, appreciation, affirmation, affection.

Techniques _____

_____

_____

Contribute

To learning environment, to school, to community, to protect environment, to help other students.

Techniques _____

_____

_____

Step 5: Involve parents, students, and others as partners.

Student

How is student an active participant in behavior change?

Teacher-student conference?	Yes _____	No _____
Student Action Plan?	Yes _____	No _____
Teacher-student-parent conference?	Yes _____	No _____

Other _____

Parent/ Guardian

What communication and involvement has occurred?

Parent-teacher discipline conference?	Yes _____	No _____
School Action Plan sent home?	Yes _____	No _____
Home Action Plan developed?	Yes _____	No _____

Specific support for School Action Plan:

_____

Others

Who else should be involved?_____ How?_____

Who can assist student?_____ How?_____

Who can assist parent?_____ How?_____

The questions on this sheet will help you think about what just happened and what can be done so it doesn't happen again. Please answer the questions honestly and with as much detail as possible. Glib or sarcastic responses will not be accepted.

My name is _____ Today's date is _____

Right now the time of day is_____

1. What did I do that got me into trouble?_____

_____

_____

_____

2. What did I want to happen? (Check all the answers that fit.)

_____ I wanted to be in charge of what was happening.

_____ I wanted to challenge the teacher's authority.

_____ I wanted to avoid doing my work.

_____ I wanted to be sent home.

_____ I wanted to be noticed by the teacher.

_____ I wanted to be noticed by the other kids.

_____ I wanted to get out of work I didn't think I could do correctly.

_____ I wanted to get even with someone.

Is there anything else I wanted?

I wanted _____

_____

I wanted _____

_____

3. Did I get what I wanted?

Yes, because _____

_____

No because _____

_____

4. Could I have gotten what I wanted in any other way?

Yes, I could have _____

_____

No, because _____

_____

5. What could I do so this won't happen again?

I could _____

I could _____

I could _____

6. This is what I am willing to do differently the next time:

_____

I will _____

I will _____

7. The name of a person who could help me do what I'm willing to do is _____
(People who might help include a teacher, counselor, peer mediator, principal, friend, family member, classmate.)

The way this person could help me is by _____

_____

8. This is what I could do to feel more capable, connected, and contributing:

I would feel more capable if I _____

_____

I would feel more connected if I _____

_____

I could contribute by _____

_____

9. This is what the school could do to help me feel more capable, connected, and contributing:

The school could help me feel more capable by _____

_____

The school could help me feel more connected by _____

_____

The school could help me contribute by _____

_____

Child _____ Teacher _____ Date _____

Step 1: Pinpoint and describe the child's behavior.

Behavior   Occurred how often?   Goal

1. _____

2. _____

3. _____

Step 2: Identify the goal.

_____

_____

_____

_____

Step 3: Choose interventions to stop the misbehavior. *When using consequences, be specific about what, where, and when the consequences will occur.*

_____

_____

_____

_____

_____

_____

Step 4: Select encouragement strategies to satisfy the need to belong and to build self-esteem.

Capable   _____

                _____

                _____

Connect   _____

                _____

Contribute   _____

                _____

An Administrator's Guide to Cooperative Discipline

This blueprint for implementing Cooperative Discipline schoolwide is filled with practical strategies for creating a positive learning environment and improving communication. Includes a management action plan, detailed instructions for the teacher "buy-in" session, funding ideas, and ideas on evaluation. Also offers a fifteen-minute video, forms, transparency masters, and handouts.

Cooperative Discipline Videos

This three-video set features real teachers and students in real classrooms. They include an overview video that introduces the Cooperative Discipline approach—plus a video on prevention and one on intervention. Available for elementary and secondary grades.

Cooperative Discipline Implementation Guide

The Cooperative Discipline Implementation Guide contains comprehensive resources for staff development, including a variety of inservice formats, handouts, transparency masters, experiential activities, instructional tip sheets—and much more.

Cooperative Discipline Posters

Ten full-color posters help you reinforce the Cooperative Discipline philosophy. Also provided are activity ideas for introducing the concepts to students.

Bringing Home Cooperative Discipline

Keep parents informed about your school's Cooperative Discipline approach with this easy-to-read booklet. It's a great way to strengthen the home-school bond, stimulate parental support for your Cooperative Discipline program, and help parents address misbehavior and build self-esteem.

Responsible Kids in School and at Home: The Cooperative Discipline Way

This six-part video series is designed for K-12 staff development and school improvement. It's filled with essential information and practical answers to problems teachers and parents face with irresponsible, disruptive, and violent behavior.

For a catalog with a complete listing of our inservice programs, please call AGS at 1-800-328-2560.